RADICAL CHANGE

A CHRISTIAN'S RESPONSE TO SECULAR HUMANISM

SCOTT LEONE

EQUIP PRESS

Colorado Springs

Radical Change
Copyright © 2021 Scott Leone

All rights reserved. No part of this publication may be reproduced, distributed, or transmitted in any form or by any means, without prior written permission.

Unless otherwise noted, all Scripture quotations are taken from the Christian Standard Bible® Copyright © 2017 by Holman Bible Publishers. Used by permission. Christian Standard Bible® and CSB® are federally registered trademarks of Holman Bible Publishers.

First Edition: June 2021
Radical Change / Scott Leone
Paperback ISBN: 978-1-951304-52-2
eBook ISBN: 978-1-951304-53-9

TABLE OF CONTENTS

Preface 1
Introduction 2
Radical Change 3
The Universe 5
The Nature of Mankind 8
Body and Soul 11
Culture 14
Faith and Science 17
Authority 21
Relevance 25
Here and Now 27
A Better Way 29
Institutional Advancement 31
Blame Game 34
Particulars 37
Different Standards 41
Knowing God 44
Radical Humanism 47
Truth and Culture 49
Church 52
A Father's Love 55
Rescue Mission – Day One 58
Rescue Mission – Day Two 60
Rebuttal 62
Live and Let Live 66
Decision Time 69
Postface 71
Postlude – A Message to Scientists 72
Appendix – Notes and Comments 78
Summary Remarks 101
Personal Testimony of Salvation 103

RADICAL CHANGE

A CHRISTIAN'S RESPONSE TO SECULAR HUMANISM

SCOTT LEONE

PREFACE

If you are like me, you have encountered directly or indirectly the debates between Christians and secular humanists. By secular humanists, I refer not only to atheists (people who reject God's existence), but to people who reject God's relevance in culture and society. They see human knowledge and discovery as focusing primarily on science and technology for the betterment of the human condition. Life focuses upon the human species and its survival.

If you consider yourself a secular humanist, then this book was written to you. I hope upon reading it you will come to see a Christian's perspective on life. I say this because the most important Person in the universe is God. Knowing Him is the essence of true salvation and is the meaning of life.

And I hope you will sense my sincerity in this story. This is not about trying to win an argument but about doing good to others, about giving people hope in a weary world. Nor am I attempting to answer all the issues between Christians and humanists. My desire is to point people to Jesus Christ, the Savior of the world, by a sincere response to some of the honest questions raised by humanists toward Christianity and religion in general.

I have experienced directly and indirectly the issues debated in this story. So, the response of the Christian character in the story represents the answers I have come to over the years while pondering these things myself and learning from others. I acknowledge the many other Christians who have labored to develop these responses as well, and thus aided me in my understanding. Standing on the shoulders of others, so to speak, I have come to see things more clearly over the years.

Therefore, I am led to thank God for the marvelous ways He guides those who love Him.

INTRODUCTION

Secular humanism is a powerful persuasion in the world today. It has given rise to numerous philosophical groups over the last few centuries. It has found strength and motivation from Enlightenment and Darwinian thought. It remains a force that shapes modern society.

This book is a fictional story of the interaction of a committed humanist, Lee, a college student, and an unidentified Christian (whose words always appear in bold type). They meet on several occasions, always at a certain bench on Lee's college campus. There they become engaged in some intense back-and-forth discussion and debate.

As in all such situations, each side presents their arguments. However, in the end, as with all such discussions, individuals are left with a choice and the consequences of that choice.

The debate is important primarily because it touches upon the eternal good of souls. Furthermore, people often talk past each other in these types of debates. So, I attempt not to do that by having the two main characters interact in a respectful way. Yes, they disagree, and at times they challenge each other. But the debate is borne out of honesty, not rancor or hatred.

My intent is to present a Christian response to secular humanism and to proclaim to the reader the wonderful riches of God's love in Jesus Christ. I make no attempt to hide the criticisms and challenges of humanism toward Christianity, nor the challenging claims of Christianity toward humanism. My hope is that you will seriously consider those Christian claims. Doing so will radically change your life now and into eternity.

RADICAL CHANGE

The story begins when a Christian meets a man named Lee on a college campus. The Christian begins to interact with Lee, engaging him in an effort to get to know him and reveal Jesus Christ to him.

"Hi, how are you?"

"I'm fine," replied Lee.

"Where are you heading?"

"I'm president of the Humanist Club on campus," said Lee. "We have a meeting tonight. Would you like to join us?"

"May I ask, what do you mean by humanism?"

"Humanism," said Lee, "is a broad term that reflects that all people belong to one human family and we try to see the world from that perspective. Art, science, history, even religion is seen from the perspective of what is common to all humans. So, we emphasize that commonality."

"I see. Is this something new?"

"Well," replied Lee, "the club is fairly new, but the idea of humanism goes back hundreds of years, even to the ancient Greeks."

"Tell me about your club. Do you have a creed? What do you talk about?"

"Well, we don't really have a creed that is fixed," said Lee. "Humanistic ideals have evolved with time. Hopefully, they are improving.

"We have sister clubs at different colleges, and occasionally we get together for conferences. Our club meets regularly to discuss the problems of the world."

"So, you see the world as needing improvement. In what ways?"

"There's poverty and ignorance, for example," said Lee. "There's also disease, inequalities, prejudice, bigotry. There's also war and violence."

"So, you think by humanism you can rid the world of all these problems?"

"Yes, bit by bit," said Lee. "Although it will take many generations."

"Why do you think these problems still exist today? Why haven't thousands of years of human life solved them?"

"Well, there's been a lot of ignorance," replied Lee. "But technology has changed the world like never before. We now have capabilities no one ever dreamed of just a few years ago."

"But hasn't there always been ignorance and war and prejudice and bigotry? Are you saying those are matters for technology to solve?"

"No," replied Lee, a bit defensively. "It's just that technology now makes more change possible, even necessary. The old ways, like traditional religions, cannot meet the needs of a technological world."

"**You mention religion. Aren't religions trying to address issues of the heart? And aren't those the real issues that cause the problems in the first place?**"

"Yah," said Lee. "But the heart needs education. That's where technology comes in."

"**So, if people are just better educated, then these problems will be solved?**"

"Yes, kind of," said Lee. "Education removes ignorance and enables people to better understand each other."

"**Then, doesn't it depend on what people are taught? Isn't education mostly about ideas, as well as facts?**"

"Sure, ideas are important," said Lee. "But ideas evolve. Old ideas aren't working. They're not fixing the problems. Humanism is a quest for better ideas to solve problems."

"**So, you think your ideas, or the ideas of humanists, will fix the problems?**"

"Yes, collectively," replied Lee. "Together our ideas will be superior to the ideas of the past. For example, history demonstrates how a few men in the past dominated others by their religious beliefs. We think that a more collective understanding of life will better serve humanity."

"**But you want the beliefs of humanists to dominate now, don't you?**"

"We represent the majority," said Lee, "not just some minority religion."

"**Billions of people are religious, but I guess you think you're still the majority?**"

"They are suffering from the ignorance I'm talking about," said Lee. "So, they are part of the problem. They need to embrace change, radical change!

"Religions are tools to quiet the masses. They keep people happy, contented. But serious, modern intellectuals reject religion as myths that served a purpose that's now outdated."

"**So, changing people's hearts for the better is outdated?**"

"No," said Lee, "just religion is outdated."

"**Okay, why don't we compare ideas? You tell me your ideas and let's see how they compare to Christian ideas. After all, aren't we both trying to solve modern problems and meet modern needs?**"

THE UNIVERSE

"Okay," replied Lee. "Foundationally, we say the universe is self-existent and not created. We think that matter and energy have always existed and are oscillating between different states over billions of years through a process of evolution.

"So, we don't need a god of any kind to help us. Science is helping us understand ourselves and our universe. With time, we will understand all the processes that have produced life and reality as we know it.

"Religious myths aren't necessary anymore. Science is clarifying reality for us and our understanding is growing all the time."

"So, you believe all this came about through time and forces or processes that humans don't fully understand yet?"

"Yes," said Lee. "And science is getting closer all the time to a more complete understanding. Religious myths aren't necessary to help us understand the universe anymore. Those myths are too simplistic."

"I see. You call religion a myth, but it sounds to me like you believe that Father Time and Mother Nature got together, and poof, here you are!"

"No, it's not like that," said Lee.

"Why not? Isn't Father Time just the endless cycles of self-existence you refer to? And isn't Mother Nature just the unknown force or process you yet hope to discover? And isn't the combination of those two your explanation for life?"

"Well, you make it sound like a fairytale," said Lee.

"Yes, and aren't you trying to make religion sound like a fairytale?"

"But we have science to back us up," responded Lee.

"No. You have faith that science will back you up. You believe that science will one day figure it all out. You have your own religion here, based on faith. But it sounds to me like a fairytale."

"You're just twisting my words," said Lee. "You don't understand."

"Sure, I understand. You want to make traditional religions like Christianity sound like a fairytale, but you won't look at yourself and how what you believe sounds like a fairytale."

"Christians aren't standing on science," said Lee. "They're standing on a book written by men, privileged men, who used religion to dominate others."

"Okay, wait, let's not get into the fact of institutional privileges in the scientific community. Let's not go down the path of their dogmatic prejudice or how they can bully others. Let's stick with this, that you want

to accept by faith a universe without God and reject that Christians accept by faith a universe created by God. Don't you think Christians fully expect that science has and will continue to vindicate God?"

"What do you mean by vindicate God?" asked Lee.

"I mean Christians believe that scientific interpretation will ultimately affirm, not contradict, the view that God designed and created all things. Christian scientists throughout the centuries have made many great discoveries. Galileo, Kelvin, Newton, Maxwell, to name a few, made great discoveries and never felt the need to abandon their faith. Rather, their faith in God gave them hope for a better understanding of all things.

"How can you be sure there is any consistent meaning in your universe without God that evolves cyclically in never ending periods of time?"

"I don't need to be sure," said Lee. "I just know there's no God. If there was, then why doesn't He reveal Himself to us?"

"God did reveal Himself. By creation and by His Son, Jesus Christ."

"Let's not get into that," replied Lee. "You Christians take the Bible too literally. You think the world is only a few thousand years old. Science has proven it to be billions of years old, and the universe as we know it is even older."

"I do have a problem with that word 'proven' that you just used. Science theorizes that the earth and universe are billions of years old. No one can *prove* that. Scientists can interpret what they see and measure, but they cannot go back in time to observe how and when it all took place."

"But the entire Genesis story is bogus," said Lee. "It reads like a fairytale. I've not studied it too much, but I know even Christians disagree on how old the earth is and how to interpret the events of Genesis chapter one. Some say it's history, others poetry. If you can't agree among yourselves, how can you expect scientists to take you seriously?

"Study modern physics. Scientists can show you the universe is old, not young."

"Look, Christians may disagree about the age of the universe. But don't think that the debate is final. No one has proven an old universe. Scientists have theories, but that's all they are. In any case, some Christians do believe in an old universe. But they still believe God created it out of nothing and created all life.

The Bible treats the days of creation in Genesis chapter one as days. They are never treated as poetry in the Bible, but as history. If there is any poetry in Genesis chapter one, it's God who is the Poet in how He chose

to create. He took delight in creating. And the order He did it in demonstrates a young earth. He created plants *before* He created the Sun. God is speaking to us through the order of creation. He is demonstrating that its existence is entirely dependent upon Him and His power and will."

"I suppose then that you don't believe in the Big Bang?" asked Lee. "Science can observe it through astronomy. There's ample evidence for it."

"God spoke all things into existence. Out of nothing, God created. Call it the Big Bang if you want to, but what science observes today is the remnant of His voice that spoke all things into existence.

"Who can imagine the wisdom and power it took for God to do that? Creation reveals something about the greatness of God. It speaks to us that way.

"Is it so hard to accept that there are things science doesn't yet understand about God's creation? You're willing to accept that idea with respect to a secular view of things, why not with a biblical view? Why not give God credit for the beauty and uniqueness of the way He created things? Let God be God and learn from His pattern of creation and His power in doing it. Be in awe of Him and discover that He is the un-created Creator, and you are His creation.

"From that perspective life takes on a whole new meaning!"

THE NATURE OF MANKIND

"Well, we're not going to agree about the origin of the universe," said Lee. "But won't you agree that mankind has formed out of a process of evolution? Don't you think science has shown that?"

"I think science has shown that creatures can evolve, but it hasn't shown that monkeys turned into men. Evolution of a species points to design, not random mutations."

"Oh, come one," said Lee. "You're not going to tell me that God made all this diversity? There's no rhyme or reason to it. It's so complex and so diverse and yet it gives evidence of a common origin that has evolved into that complexity.

"Scientists are noticing the connections in DNA that points conclusively to evolution. So, yah, men did evolve from monkeys — apes to be more precise."

"I see the symphony of harmony in all of life. It's amazing. And to me it points to God. I see His design in atoms and planets; I see it in single cell creatures and complex animals. There is a symphony of harmony that should point you to a great, wise, and awesome Designer God who delights in all He made.

"Your idea of God is too small. You cannot conceive of the wisdom of a personal Being so great that all this is due to His power. You would rather fall back on time and unknown forces or processes to explain it all. But in doing so you rob God of the glory He deserves."

"If there was such a God," asked Lee, "then why doesn't He show Himself. You say He did, but I don't see it. All I see is a world whose causes and effects can be explained by natural forces.

"You say my idea of God is too small, but maybe your view of nature is too limited. Why not random mutations? If all we can observe are the forces of nature, then that's all we must go on. I don't see God in that."

"I understand that the idea of unlimited mutations is a tempting thought as to how life came about. You observe species adapting to new situations. You see certain forces of nature and look to them to explain things. It seems so logical that everything just evolved on its own by those same things. It's alluring to find the solution to mysteries you don't understand in things you do. I get that.

"But look carefully at yourself. Don't you see God in people? Why do people ask questions no other creature asks? Why do people get excited about ideas of art, science, philosophy, music, and so on? Why are humans so fundamentally different than animals? Could it be that God has revealed something of Himself through humans?

"Christianity teaches that men and women are created in the *image of God*. That's why people are so different."

"I think humans have evolved further than other animals," replied Lee. "That's all it is. It's just more evolution. Genetics teaches us that humans are linked to apes and we have evolved beyond them."

"Common genetics can also point to a common design. But if human advancement is just more evolution, then why aren't there other creatures on earth that have at least some of the same advanced abilities humans have? I grant that God gave all creatures wonderful abilities and intelligence. But why aren't they developing technology like people do? Why don't they record history, study the stars, improve on farming or housing, talk and reason the way humans do? Rather, we see animals — including apes — content to do the same things over and over, as if they were made that way, without the created — God-imitating — abilities that humans have?"

"I'm sure there are advanced life forms elsewhere in the universe," said Lee. "We just haven't discovered them yet. Maybe humans came here from alien worlds. There are possibilities other than God."

"I see. There you go again expressing your belief that science will save the day and prove your faith is right. But science cannot explain how mankind emerged so different from other life forms. To me, it points to God and to His desire to reveal something about Himself through mankind."

"I still say evolution holds the key," said Lee. "But I see your point. You want to assign human uniqueness to a Designer. I don't see that."

"Okay, but people are not the only way God has revealed Himself. Christians believe God sent His Son, Jesus Christ. God Himself was in His Son. So, the Son revealed God in a very personal way."

"Are you saying that Jesus was God?" asked Lee. "I admit He was a good man and a moral teacher, but that's all."

"Why is it so hard for you to believe that God revealed Himself through Jesus? You complain that God hasn't revealed Himself. Then, when I say He has, you reject it. So, what you really want is for God to submit to your way of revealing Himself? Don't you think that's a little much? And doesn't it make sense that if God did create people in His own image and they needed help that He would in some way *personally* help them?"

"Anybody can say he is God's Son," replied Lee. "How do we know what Jesus said is true?"

"Yes, that's the next way I'd like to show you how God has revealed Himself. God has revealed Himself through the Bible. Over many years, God inspired certain men whom He specially called and gifted to reveal His personal Being and will through them. And they wrote down that revelation. So, through the Bible everyone can know by recorded revelation who Jesus is.

"Again, doesn't it make sense that if God revealed Himself in people and that He came to them through His Son, that He would also provide a way to make it *certain* to them by a revealed record? That's what the Bible is — God's assurance that what He has revealed about Himself is true."

"There are lots of other books that claim to be from God?" replied Lee. "How can we know which one is right? You see how arbitrary it becomes? Anyone can claim a book that's from God."

"True, but only one truth is God's Truth. The proof is in the book itself, not in the claims people make. The Bible claims to be God's word all through it. What's more, those claims are substantiated by those who humbly read it. There is no book like it. It spans thousands of years of history and was written over a period of about fifteen hundred years. It has been thoroughly tested in the crucible of human experience. No other book is like that. It is not the expressions or claims of one man. It is the consistent and cumulative work of many who were expressing the same consistency because God inspired them."

"You can't prove that," replied Lee.

"Do I have to? I'm giving you a well-reasoned argument on how God has revealed Himself. You wanted that and here it is. I say, beyond a reasonable doubt, I have answered your question. You require more proof, but you reject the proof I'm giving you."

"I have to go," said Lee. "I'm going to be late for my meeting."

BODY AND SOUL

A few days later, Lee was walking on campus and came upon the same person he had met before on his way to the Humanist Club meeting.

"Hi!"

"Hi," replied Lee.

"How did your meeting go the other night?"

"Fine," said Lee.

"What did you discuss?"

"We had a guest speaker," began Lee a little tenuously. "She spoke about how naturalistic processes have resulted in human consciousness. She explained that we are complex organisms, and, in that complexity, there emerges our conscious awareness of ourselves and our surroundings. I thought it was great!"

"Interesting. So, she was saying that people are just atoms and chemical processes and not a body and soul?"

"Yes," said Lee. "That's about it. And there is no scientific evidence for a soul. We are atoms working in a complex way that causes the emergence of consciousness. The notion of the soul emerges from that same consciousness. And, yes, that consciousness results from very complex chemical processes."

"Well, isn't that a depressing thought. I guess a person's activities, decisions, likes, and dislikes, are all just the products of what they had for breakfast that day. Is that about it?"

Lee smiled and said, "No, it's much more complex than that. It took many years for our body to form as it has. My personality, likes, and dislikes have developed over many years, and my body's ability to do that has evolved over millions of years."

"I was being sarcastic, of course. But still, decisions are just chemical reactions, right?"

"I guess so," said Lee. "There is input that is processed and the result is conditioned upon other previous inputs."

"That's interesting. Then let me ask you, why do you teach people knowledge?"

"Knowledge is part of the preconditioning," replied Lee.

"Does the content of the knowledge really matter? I mean, if a certain set of information will produce one result and another set another result, then why does it matter which set is taught?"

"We want people to know the truth," said Lee. "Otherwise, the species will be weakened by bad information."

"Oh, so it's good to save the species. That's your goal?"

"Yes," said Lee exasperatedly, "of course it is!"

"Why?"

"What do you mean, why?" asked Lee. "It's built into all species to survive."

"Why?"

"Because it is!" shouted Lee in disbelief, throwing his hands into the air. "Species want to survive."

"Let me put it another way. You are assuming that it's good to teach a certain set of knowledge and not good to teach another set of knowledge, because you think that's how best to survive. Yet, you admit you're just atoms and chemical reactions. How can chemistry define survival?"

"What do you mean?" asked Lee.

"Wouldn't chemical reactions tend toward the lowest use of energy? Wouldn't they tend toward a simpler state? Wouldn't irreversible processes eventually take complex reactions to a simpler, less complex set of reactions as energy is expended? In other words, how would mere chemical reactions develop complex systems that want to survive or are somehow conscious of survival unless there was some purposeful design involved?"

"I not sure I understand what you're saying," said Lee.

"I'm sorry. Let me say it another way. First, if people are just atoms and chemical reactions, then it doesn't matter what state they're in. It's all meaningless. A rock is more stable than a person, so is dirt. Why worry about knowledge or survival? Wouldn't the state of dirt be better?

"Second, if consciousness is just an emergence from chemical complexity, then what concern do you have for someone else or for the species? What does it really matter? Who are you to say human complexity is more meaningful than a pile of dirt, or a rock, or a burning star?

"You act like God by elevating life to a special place. Why? Aren't you just playing God? Aren't you just acting like God by trying to determine your own meaning and reality?"

Lee was silent for a moment and then said, "Why can't you just accept that we're all just products of random forces and evolution? Why do we have to have a God? My life is meaningful to me without that."

"If people are body only, and do not have a soul that interacts with that body, then life is meaningless. Everyone is just meaningless chemical reactions. I fail to see why any set of knowledge matters versus another.

"What I'm getting at is that consciousness points to design. Even if people use artificial intelligence to create a kind of consciousness, it's still by design. God is the Great Designer who gave all life its unique consciousness. And He elevated human consciousness to the special place where it can actually come to know God because He gave people a soul as well as a body. That soul distinguishes humans from animals and enables them to know God."

CULTURE

"Look," said Lee, "we are all products of our environment. One person is shaped one way and another person another way by the experiences and culture they are in. Those experiences produce meaning to each individual. No experience is more valid than any other. They're all just different.

"And, as people live, science informs their experiences. We add to our understanding by scientific knowledge. I'm not trying to act like a god or something. I'm just trying to make sense of world."

"Okay, if people are products of their environment then what implication does that have for ethics? How can mere chemical reactions determine right and wrong?"

"Again," said Lee, "it's about survival. My consciousness determines my will to survive, as does the consciousness of others. Right and wrong follow from a proper desire for the species to survive."

"Would you say that Hitler was wrong? Is it wrong to remove weak people from the gene pool? I mean, if they hinder the survival of others and ethics are just the product of certain chemical reactions, then why not? Or what about rape? Aren't rapists just responding to powerful hormonal reactions inside them? In other words, if it's all just experiences and culture and the work of chemicals trying to survive, then ethics have no true meaning, do they?"

"Sure," said Lee, "ethics matter as each culture determines them. Hitler determined one ethic; others opposed it. He lost; they won."

"So, you wouldn't say Hitler was wrong or evil?"

"Right and wrong," replied Lee, "are cultural constructs. If Hitler had won, then we'd all be happy Nazis, I guess!" Lee paused, then continued. "But Hitler was wrong because the broader social context opposed him. He was wrong because his efforts hurt the broader survival of the species.

"The same goes for murder or rape. Those activities hurt the overall survival of the species."

"Well, at least you're trying to be consistent. You know as well as I that Hitler was evil and wrong and had to be stopped. To me, your purely naturalistic worldview cannot explain Hitler except from the framework of survival. Yet, Hitler could justify himself on that same basis! So, you can only make an ethical statement that's relative to some temporal social context or to your idea of survival.

"Yet why does survival matter? Maybe the world would be better off

without humans to ruin it?"

"I see where you are going," replied Lee. "But naturalistic forces make all the movements of history. It's just a battle of wills. One assembly of chemicals asserts itself on another set. That's life!

"Ethics also flows out of our will to survive. That battle of wills is also a battle for survival. Right and wrong become constructs of that survival. I know Hitler was wrong because he threatened our survival, our freedom, our liberty as humans to determine our own destiny."

"Wow! I'm glad you're being honest again. But what a stark reality you paint. It sure doesn't seem like that view is ever going to solve the problems mankind faces. If culture alone, or even culture informed somehow by science, shapes and molds people, then we're again left with conflict and a battle of wills for survival, certainly not peace and harmony. Yet isn't that the picture of human history? And, ironically, especially over the last few hundred years or so, when certain secular ideas have flourished."

"Look," said Lee, "science also informs our ethics. Consider the contributions of science to our understanding of the mind. Mental diseases can cause people to do things that contradict the survival of the species. Furthermore, science helps us understand the fundamental equality of people. We're all built the same, yet with differing abilities. Ethical judgments can flow out of that understanding, but it doesn't require God to get there."

"I agree that science can and does inform our ethics. I don't discount psychology and physiology as making contributions to understanding human behavior.

"However, the problem with depending on science for ethical standards is that you are still leaving those decisions to people. Ethics become self-referential. You set the standards. It becomes like a self-fulfilling prophecy to say this is right and that is wrong. Right and wrong can change. Absolutes become relativistic rules that fade away or are changed. Who knows where a culture will end up when people determine their own ethical standards?

"I'm not suggesting that all ethical decisions are clear-cut or easy to arrive at. But I'm saying that without a standard *outside* of humanity, ethics become merely choices and opinions that change. That seems to be a very convenient approach for dodging moral responsibility and for getting one's own way! Thus, it results in a battle of wills, not peace and harmony."

"So," asked Lee, "you think there is something fundamental to human beings that makes us act the way we do? You think there's something more than culture and experience?"

"Yes. Now you see where I'm going. As I said before, Christians believe humans to be created to reflect the image of God. Therefore, God's character and ways are deeply imprinted within all people. That's why you inherently know Hitler was evil and that rape is wrong. It's not naturalistic or chemical reactions that tell you that. It's God's design!"

"I'll have to think about it," said Lee, as he sat down on a bench.

FAITH AND SCIENCE

After Lee sat down, he thought for a moment. Then he said, "Science may not have all the answers now, but it is the only way we can truly know anything. We explore, we observe, we reason things out, and we act upon what we've learned. That's science. What you say is faith, not science. That's why I cannot accept it. Faith involves too much subjective opinion."

"Are you saying that science and faith are opposites or incompatible?"

"Yes," said Lee. "Faith involves too much subjective opinion. Science can measure things and know things by that measurement. We can therefore learn and advance only by science."

"Isn't that a statement of faith?"

"No," said Lee, "because I can observe that it's true."

"So, you discount the observations of others, just because they are not your observations?"

"What do you mean?" asked Lee.

"Some people have observed miracles, supernatural events, things that don't happen every day, but that God performed to reveal some truth about Himself. These people observed these things and wrote them down. It's not unreasonable to accept their testimony when your faith agrees with theirs."

"That's just it," said Lee, "it's a matter of their faith and your faith. I don't see it, so I don't believe it."

"So, you deny what you don't see?"

"Yes," said Lee.

"But you're willing to believe that one day science will fully discover everything?"

"Yes, it will," relied Lee.

"And that's not a statement of faith? You see, you cannot truly know anything without faith. Faith embraces the unknown with a confidence in something. Your confidence is in science and you embrace the unknown believing that science will give you the answer. Christians have confidence in God and embrace the unknown believing God knows all things and will guide them and help them as they trust Him.

"To you, science is like a personal deity that helps you. To Christians, God is a personal Being who helps them. God created all that science observes, but God is beyond all that He created. He is able to break into His universe in ways people may not understand but that are consistent with who He is."

"Science is all we need to solve our problems," replied Lee. "We see it now, advancing us. We don't see God or His relevance in the world. All we need is what science already gives us.

"Our own investigation of the world enlightens us enough. We study, we learn, and we apply that knowledge to life. It all makes simple sense. Why complicate things by bringing in opinions about God?"

"By saying that science is all you need, aren't you looking self-referentially and expecting answers from yourself? You say the 'thing only exists' and so 'only the thing' can help you. Christians believe 'God is the only Creator' and so 'only Creator God' can help them. You take matter and make it God. Christians take God for who He is. The difference is that God is not the creation! God is not the stuff He made; He is far beyond it.

"You then end up honoring yourself as the one who helps yourself! Christians end up honoring God. You become like God because you become the one who determines all things. Christians say that's God's ultimate role, and He helps people understand His universe through the things He has revealed.

"One way God reveals things is through science. His orderliness, His wisdom in how things work, His power and grandeur are revealed in some way through the creation, and science is how He helps people understand it. Science is one of the tools God created to know more about Him.

"So, when God reveals Himself in thoughts that are written down or by the person of His Son, we use our minds to know it and our faith to accept it. You do the same thing. You use your mind to know things you read or observe, and your faith accepts it.

"What I'm saying is that faith and science are inseparable. You cannot have science without faith. Let me put it this way: faith and reason are like two sides of the same coin. They are not contradictory, they are complementary.

"But what's so important to understand is God gave both. Science observes, but faith accepts it. There is no other way of knowing anything.

"And it is good science to study God's revelation in creation and in the Bible and use faith to accept what you learn. That's how you can know it's true."

"How can you say faith and science go together like that?" asked Lee. "I don't understand. Objective reality is one thing, subjective is another. What's objective is outside me. What's subjective is inside me. That's how science and faith differ. I can observe what's outside of me, so that defines reality for me and everyone else."

"Have you heard of quantum mechanics?"

"Sure," said Lee.

"Then you know that states or properties of atoms involve probabilities and uncertainties. Yet, those probabilities and uncertainties are not unreasonable because they can be used to explain how some things work.

"So why is faith any different? Let's take your secular perspective for a moment. If people are just atoms and chemical reactions, then faith, too, is a process within them that has mechanical, perhaps even Quantum, roots. If faith exists, then it is produced by processes that are just as real as so-called reason.

"I'm not suggesting that faith is a purely naturalistic process. I believe faith is connected to the soul. Faith encompasses more than mechanical processes — which might explain why some people want to deny the necessity and validity of faith as relevant to the issues of life.

"Faith is especially unique in humans because God created mankind to love and trust Him in a very personal and special way. Such faith in God is real, and it moves God to act on behalf of those who love Him.

"Furthermore, real faith implies trust in something you don't necessarily see directly. It involves a conviction of the reality of things unseen. So, faith involves a confidence that something is true and a conviction of its truthfulness even when you don't see all the details.

"All I'm saying is that faith and reason operate together. They cannot be separated. What you call pure reason based on observation, I call a combination of reason and faith that your observations both hold true now and in all circumstances."

"But here's the difference between us," replied Lee. "I can measure what I believe. I can observe it. I cannot observe God."

"How about this? The measurement (observation) of anything causes an effect in you and that effect is faith — the belief that the measurement is true. That's why you accept it."

"Okay, let's say I grant that," said Lee. "Then I believe in what I observe. You believe in what you don't observe — namely, God!"

"Wait a minute. You are again suggesting that we don't observe God in the world. That's an unwarranted statement. As I said before, I see God in the things He created. I see His wisdom and power. I see God in people as they reflect His image. And I see God through His revelation in the Bible, especially of His Son, Jesus. These are all observations. Granted you deny they are valid, but that's on you. It's completely rational to believe in God through what He has truly revealed.

"So, things that happen that are called supernatural that have been observed and recorded in the Bible can be reasonably accepted by faith because they happened. The fact that you or I didn't see them happen doesn't make them false. They happened. People recorded them with God's help. Now we can read about them and accept that testimony. And God will do much more supernatural activity when Jesus comes again."

Lee said, "So, you say, 'God and the Bible and creation,' and I say, 'nature' and from that I accept it by faith and live. Is that what you're saying?"

"Yes, basically, that's it. Only I'm adding that there's no reason to think that the supernatural cannot happen. It may not be observed readily now, but it has been recorded by God's inspiration and you can accept that by faith."

AUTHORITY

"Okay," relied Lee, "you want to establish that the supernatural is valid. Let me approach this from another perspective. By what authority do you say the supernatural is valid? It seems to me that all things must be subject to scientific investigation. Science must be the final authority on what we believe or don't believe is real.

"If I just take religion by faith and yet I cannot observe its reality, then how can you expect me to rationally accept that? Prove to me first that these things are so. Show me with science as the authority. Then I can accept it.

"What is real is tangible, tactile, felt. You speak of things unseen and unknown as if it's okay just to accept them. I can't do that and be true to myself. To me such things are not necessarily real. So, I'm not willing to trust what I cannot know is real.

"Do you see my point?"

"Yes, I do. But aren't you neglecting the testimony of millions of people throughout history who can attest to the validity of their faith?"

"You're asking me to take the word of others. Lots of people attest to their version of God. Lots of people make religious claims. But I can't take them as my authority."

"Okay, let's think about authority for a moment. You trace your authority back to science. But in doing so you are assuming that there is no bias in how people interpret science.

"You see, people interpret things through the grid of their beliefs. You talk as though there is one authoritative interpretation to all scientific statements, but the fact is scientists will impose their worldview on the data. Sometimes, therefore, even scientists interpret data to make it fit their worldview."

"So you think scientists are dishonest?" asked Lee. "That seems like a convenient accusation on your part, convenient for getting your own ideas in."

"No, scientists are not dishonest. But it's human nature I'm referring to. What I'm saying is that people make decisions based upon a process that works like this:

"People have their fundamental beliefs. Perhaps they formed those beliefs from their parents or their schooling or both. Those beliefs form their worldview. They interpret the world and act and live starting from that worldview. Then they test that worldview by living their life. Think of it as scientific investigation. When they perceive that the result doesn't

match their worldview then they adjust their beliefs, or they adjust their interpretation of the investigation to make it fit their beliefs.

"The process is circular. Beliefs create a worldview, that generates behavior and an outlook on life, experience tests that behavior and outlook to validate it, then either the beliefs are fortified or changed to accommodate their experience, or their interpretation of the experience is changed to fit their beliefs!

"What this means is that without an authority that comes from God, people will place authority ultimately *upon themselves*. You call science the authority as if science is an unbiased god that can tell you what is real. I'm saying that's not true. People ultimately make *themselves* the authority by how they interpret experiences and then by what they do with that interpretation. The whole process is very self-referential. And it affirms your secular humanistic view of life. Talk about convenience.

"Now let's think about authority from a Christian's perspective. Christians make the Bible their ultimate authority for metaphysical matters. For example, science cannot go back in time to make observations. The Bible reveals origins. Science cannot define humans except by what it observes in people. The Bible reveals that humans are made in God's image, sinful, and in need of salvation. And scientific investigation ends at the grave. The Bible reveals what's coming in eternity.

"The Bible reveals what cannot be discovered scientifically. That puts the Bible is a special place as God's revelation."

"But the Bible was written by people," said Lee. "Aren't you ultimately also placing your trust in people?"

"The Bible says that all Scripture is God-breathed, literally breathed out by God's Spirit. That happened as certain men were moved by God's own Spirit to write what God wanted them to write. So, God is the ultimate author of the Bible.

"However, the writers were not just dictating words from God. They were also using their knowledge and experiences to convey God's message. That message came through a historical context and addressed historical events, but it is still God's message.

"Because it is God's message — breathed out by God's Spirit through the writers — it is relevant to people today. That's why the Bible is a valid authority today. It is God's message directly to human beings, meant to guide them to the path of eternal life and to how God created them to live."

"I suppose that your view of the Bible is one way," said Lee, "but someone else's is another way. You are still leaving yourself as the authority, aren't you? And won't Christians have the same process of circularity you described? Aren't they just going to reinterpret life to fit the Bible?"

"It's true that people differ in how they view some Bible statements. The Bible itself warns of those who will twist the Scriptures for their own purposes. But the Bible is also clear and, in many ways, simple. When people impose a philosophical grid of interpretation onto the Bible then they nullify it or make it say what they want it to say. But when people simply, honestly, and prayerfully read it, they discover that it is self-authenticating. That is, it validates itself. They come to know it is God's word."

"So," asked Lee, "if I just read the Bible, you're saying that I'll come away with believing it to be God's word? Lots of people have read the Bible and not believed it. So again, that's just your understanding but it doesn't work for everyone. Again, that's not favoring your argument."

"Many people read the Bible out of curiosity. It's not a magic formula book. You make it sound like I'm suggesting it's a magic formula to read the Bible and then suddenly you'll become a Christian. That's not what I'm saying.

"Believing must come first. One must believe that God exists and approach the Bible as God's revelation. You cannot test the living God as though He is some experiment and must submit Himself to your grilling, your scientific investigation. Rather, approach Him sincerely and honestly with all your heart through the Scriptures. Then you'll come to know Him."

"Believe the Bible and know God, or believe God and read the Bible? Sounds to me like a chicken and egg situation," said Lee. "What comes first?"

"God comes first. It is therefore completely rational to trust Him. His authority is true and foundational. He has revealed Himself through the God-breathed Scriptures. You can take Him at His word. His testimonies are completely reliable. And you will find in the Bible a lamp for your feet and a light for your path; a way to know God is real and a place to solidly rest your faith and base your living.

"Also, let me answer your comment about Christian beliefs and circularity. Yes, all beliefs are circular, as I described. But the difference is that Christians start on the solid foundation of belief in the eternal God who reveals Himself. You want to start from matter as eternal. That leaves you as the ultimate interpreter of observations, the ultimate authority, because matter only speaks *through you.* Christians humbly rest upon God through His word and therefore God is their ultimate authority, and one finds a solid place to rest their soul."

RELEVANCE

"Still," replied Lee, "even if God exists, I'm not convinced He is relevant. He's too distant, too detached. If belief in God helps you, fine. But new thought processes, or beliefs if you will, have come along and they help me live just fine. God is irrelevant to me.

"I can be a good person, get along with others, help others, whatever, without God. And science and technology are always there to help me. They are constantly progressing so I can progress too.

"If God helps you get through life then that's good for you. But don't think that we all have to accept your views.

"There are many great people in the world who have ideas that help others, and their ideas don't require God. Advances in healthcare help people live longer. New ideas free people from religious restraints.

"Religious ideas restrict; they confine us and constrict us. We're free from God and no one is going to bring us back under religious sway again. That's why humanism is so freeing. Your ideas just turn back the clock of progress!"

"What can I say but that your arguments give proof to the validity of the Bible."

"What do you mean by proof?" asked Lee.

"The Bible teaches that God made mankind good and innocent, without evil. He also gave them freedom to make choices, but those choices were bound by God's will. He required the first man and woman to trust Him and be fully devoted to Him. They were given freedom with responsibility.

"You speak as if God is only restricting people. No, God is protecting them. He gives them complete freedom within the boundaries of His will expressed by His word.

"However, there was a fallen, rebellious angel named Satan who tempted the first man and woman to disobey God. They fell into the same state of rebellion that Satan did. And all their descendants also fell. They fell from a state of innocence before God to a state that manifests disobedience to God and selfishness from even the youngest age.

"Your ideas express exactly what the Bible teaches has become of fallen human beings. There is now a rebellious spirit in people that disobeys God, won't listen to Him, and goes its own way.

"You give evidence to the validity of the biblical account of mankind."

Lee replied, "You want people to submit to your rules. You fix a set of laws from God and want everyone to obey them. That's restrictive!"

"No, it's not. Within God's laws there is complete freedom and liberty. What you want is to elevate your opinions to be law. And you strive to convince others to do the same thing.

"People can no more function without laws than city traffic can function without lights and rules of passage. Laws are fundamental to science and nature. All I'm saying is that in addition to natural laws, God has given moral laws.

"As surely as people cannot disobey the laws of nature without consequences, they cannot disobey the moral laws of nature's God without consequences.

"You talk about being good or helping people and doing so without God. But what's your reference point for goodness?"

"My reference point is culture," said Lee. "It's what the majority wants. It's what makes life intelligible and satisfying. That's the good I strive for. I can reach that satisfaction through the secular alone, without God."

"I have no doubt you can reach a feeling of self-satisfaction. But pride has a way of making a person feel right even though they may be wrong. Pride can lock a person into an insecure world of self-satisfaction. And that insecurity will drive them to lead others to the same place.

"The problem with your view that God is irrelevant is that it feeds pride and has serious consequences. So, as you try to convince others of your views, you are doing what Satan tried to do and succeeded. He drove the first man and woman away from God and toward him. That had very serious consequences for them and all their posterity. For these matters are not just about ideas, they're about eternal life and peoples' souls."

"See," said Lee, "that's why I hate religion. You just want us to feel guilty, so we'll follow your God!"

"No, that's not true. If I saw you drowning and did nothing to help you, I would be unloving and a coward. I see souls perishing by rebellion against God. Not to help them would be unloving. To help them is loving.

"The consequences of your views are eternal. You deny that, but that's not me making you feel guilty, that's just you refusing to take responsibility for your beliefs and actions."

"I'm just saying," said Lee exasperatedly, "that I don't need your God!"

"Okay, and I say you do need Him, but you don't want Him because your pride is getting in the way, hardening you toward Him."

"Pride has nothing to do with it," said Lee. "My views are intelligent!"

HERE AND NOW

Lee left the scene feeling a bit angry. But he remembered that later that night he was going to hear a visiting philosophy professor who he knew was a devoted humanist. So, as he looked forward to the session, his spirit lifted.

Lee came to the meeting and sat down. A woman stood up to introduce the guest speaker. Then the guest stood up and he began to speak.

"Long ago, as life began its journey from the so-called primordial pool, one goal has been in view — it is the development of the being in the here and now. That struggle 'to be' has produced the forces of evolution from organizational and molecular evolution to social and cultural evolution.

"As one life form met the challenges of the here and now, it adapted and changed; it learned new features and discovered better ways to survive.

"Millions and millions of life forms have come and gone. Many we likely have no record of. But theirs was a transitional contribution to a better world. Better for survival, that is. Better for satisfaction, and individual, as well as collective, development. Better for fulfillment in the here and now.

"We owe much to these unknown transitional species. Our current fulfillment and satisfaction in life emanates from their struggle to survive. We truly stand on the shoulders of others who met the challenges of the here and now in their time.

"Therefore, we can conclude that anything that distracts us from the here and now, distracts us from survival. Anything that hinders personal focus on, and cooperative effort with, the here and now endangers the human species.

"Our goal in the here and now is actually a better tomorrow. By focusing on the things that improve us today, we guarantee a better tomorrow for the next generation. And, in this grand effort we are following in the tradition of millions of years of evolution.

"However, belief in the so-called supernatural only distracts from the progress of evolution we endeavor to make. We understand why some people feel the need to have a god to help them. But we know that our present condition happened through evolutionary progress and not a god.

"Humankind will therefore progress through the development of the here and now. Today is our moment in history to shine. These halls of learning are our hallowed temples. We celebrate with joy and enthusiasm each other and our achievements that make humankind progress.

"Sure, we are taking risks. Reality itself is probabilistic. Unknown and random forces have achieved miracles, even the miracle of life. So, let us not fear to take risks to advance into the unknown, to try, to strive after human betterment.

"We are not trying to create unrealistic ideals. We want realism, and we find it on the mature path of intellectual inquiry. This bold step forward in discovery and inquiry into the basic processes of nature can only lead us to a better tomorrow.

"You young people are our hope as you embrace these humanistic goals. For you will not only achieve personal satisfaction, you will likely provide others with joys and encouragements they would not have experienced on their own.

"So, embrace the here and now. Study it. Enjoy it. Take risks in it. Explore the unknown. Develop your ideas. Let interaction with others be the crucible to test your ideas. Out of the fires of inquiry burn off the dross of ignorance so that only the pure gold of knowledge remains.

"Talk, interact, share ideas that benefit the here and now. Tomorrow will benefit from it. Evolution will produce a refinement of each generation. You and I are part of that.

"Seize the moment to advance!

"Thank you."

The room burst into applause. Lee felt affirmed and ready to go forth with renewed vigor to promote humanistic goals.

After the meeting, Lee approached the speaker and asked him, "What do you think needs to be done with traditional religions like Christianity?"

"That's an excellent question," replied the speaker. "Traditional religions can have a meaningful role in human progress only if they change. For example, certain emotions associated with spirituality must be defined by psychology. Exclusivist ideas must go. The dogmatism of religious law must be replaced with relativistic ideas that adapt more readily to the times.

"If changes, radical changes, like these don't take place in traditional religions, then they will become less relevant and more ineffective at solving the world's problems."

Lee smiled and thanked the speaker. He left the meeting rejuvenated and wishing he would encounter that person again who had argued so forcefully for the Christian worldview.

A BETTER WAY

Lee got his wish. The next day he walked by the bench he sat on the last time he spoke with that mysterious person and sure enough, there sat the Christian.

"Hi!" said Lee.

"Good morning. How are you today?"

"I'm just great," said Lee smiling. "And, last night I heard an amazing speaker that …"

"I know, I heard him too."

"You did?" inquired Lee as he sat down. "Funny, I didn't see you there. Well, what did you think? How do you respond to that?"

"When we first met, we discussed how to make the world a better place. But I ask you, how can people become all they were intended to be when they reject a major portion of what they should become? Let me explain.

"Evolution for you is a gradual process that you are convinced leads to improvement. You believe that improvement is certain because you assume people evolved from a lower state to their present higher state. You look at what you are now, and you extrapolate back in time under the assumption that things were much worse or less developed in people.

"Now, I grant you that knowledge and technology have grown immensely, even in the last few hundred years.

"But, ignoring raw knowledge and technology itself, let's focus on human nature. What if the view that mankind has evolved from a lower state to a higher state is totally backwards? What if the truth is that people have actually become worse; that they have evolved more cunning ways to deceive themselves and others, more complex ways to reject true reality and to create their own?

"Christians say that God made humans good and innocent and able to know Him, love Him, and experience Him. Through the deception of Satan, that good was ruined when the first humans disobeyed God and fell from their lofty state.

"Ever since then, it has been a downward spiral. People have advanced and enhanced ways to exalt themselves and ignore God. They have advanced in ways that have codified rebellion and cauterized conscience against that gnawing sense of the unknown eternal and the divine.

"One way they have done this is by focusing on the here and now. It sounds so appealing. It affirms that inner state of individualism that affirms self.

"However, it leaves off much of reality and is not wise. To ignore the future beyond death is to deny reality in favor of a fairytale. God will hold each person accountable for his or her actions, thoughts, and words. To ignore that is to jeopardize your future and the future of others.

"Now, that doesn't mean that people should not be concerned about the here and now. The present is very important, but not at the expense of eternity, of the future when people will stand before God to give an account of themselves.

"Don't you see? It's not just the now, it's also the future. It's both.

"That speaker was affirming what will cost people their souls. That's serious.

"You think you're concerned for the species surviving. People cannot survive rejecting God. They cannot defeat God no matter how alluring their arguments appear.

"Why shouldn't survival include eternity? Really, it does. But secular humanism leaves a person dead, buried, and gone after this life. There's no hope for eternity. The here and now is sold as all there is. You leave people high and dry, lost, without a compass or means of propulsion on into eternity.

"What hope have you to give a person on their deathbed? What words of comfort can you give for the person struggling with fears in terminal cancer?

"You see, the here and now sounds great until you face death. Then you must grit your teeth and hope you were right, and the Christian was wrong. What a way to die!

"To me that's cruel and selfish and unloving to rob people of eternal life merely to appear to fortify one's position. But isn't that human nature? People want the feeling of adulation they receive as others congratulate them for their ideas. But the harsh reality of death will steal away that joy. Only pride or ignorance will carry them peacefully into the darkness of death. For there is no hope in the view that the here and now is all there is.

"A better way is to deal with reality in its fulness. It's not just the here and now, it's also eternity."

INSTITUTIONAL ADVANCEMENT

Lee spoke up and said, "Humanism has made many institutional advancements to human life because it embraces the here and now as its only focus. Government, education, healthcare, you name it. Humanism has advanced learning and opportunity because the goal is a better life for all. It happens through society as people cooperate to make life better for everyone, *now*.

"If people are all worried about eternity, then how will they confront the challenges of today? Religion is a distraction from solving the problems of human suffering."

"No one can deny that changes are required when people suffer economic or social injustices. And I acknowledge that many non-Christians have made the world a better place. But humanists are often guilty of two things: first, taking credit for what they don't deserve, and second, blaming others for what they don't deserve.

"For example, Christians have made the world a better place economically and socially on many levels. Christian teaching of love to God and love to one's neighbor as their self is the highest ideal. That forms the basis for a better society.

"Christians started many of the great institutions of learning and funded the arts and encouraged learning of all kinds. When the church overstepped its authority, reformations have taken place. There have been self-corrections in the Church to return to the fundamental principles of God's law and grace.

"Christianity has lifted mankind from the cruel grips of all kinds of tyranny. And, before Christ came, the Jews led the world in revealing a God of law and love. No other culture has had such a god. All the false gods are impersonal, cruel, slave drivers, or merely there to affirm one's self and desires.

"Christianity and the Bible teach a God of love and law, of grace, mercy, and yet wrath. As people experience God's love and forgiveness, their heart is moved to love and forgive others. Grace from God begets grace in the Christian's heart toward others. That spirit of grace forms the basis for true equality and humility.

"Look at history. Every humanistic philosophy has evolved into either a totalitarian form of government or a socialistic one that pushes God aside. Then the few always end up dominating the many. You end up preaching a fairytale, a lie. It never works out that way you claim it will because you're not founded upon God's grace or God's law. You make your own law, you become your own judge, you end up playing God!

"You claim that common good is your goal, but it always ends up with a few elites who dominate the masses.

"Has it ever occurred to you that the true opium of the masses is the socialistic humanism you espouse? Yes, that idea that a privileged enlightened few will save everyone from themselves, play God, and meet all their needs. That's the true elixir that keeps the masses in line.

"The real change that will affect culture and society for good is the radical change of the human heart. When people experience God's love and grace through Jesus, they become like God to others, not as their lords and masters, but as examples of God's love and grace."

Lee interjected with a smirk, "I don't know any Christians so full of love and grace."

"Okay, maybe you don't, maybe many Christians are immature or don't fully understand the gospel of Jesus. But don't throw the baby out with the bath water. Don't reject Christianity because some Christians fail. Recognize that Christians don't claim to be perfect or better, just forgiven and free from sin's dominion over them, not free from sin altogether.

"Christians fail, but God is working in them through the Bible and a growing understanding of Jesus. Christians are human 'becomings.' They are changing.

"No Christian earns salvation by being a good person. But Christians strive to be a good person out of gratitude to God for having been given salvation as a free and unmerited gift."

"But what about all those Christians who don't live up to what the Bible says?" asked Lee, "Doesn't it matter how you live as a Christian?"

"Yes, it matters. I'm saying that Christians are not saved on the basis of how they live. They should live as a response to God's grace, not to earn that grace. Grace is God's gift. You cannot earn a gift.

"Look, if God graded people on a curve, everyone would fail because of sin; no one would be saved. Rather, God saves those who humbly put their trust in Jesus as their Savior from sin. That's grace — God does for sinners what they cannot do for themselves and gives to them what they don't deserve.

"Living the Christian life is a response to God's grace. Yet, Christians are growing and learning. They are not perfect. For you to demand perfection misunderstands grace and is an unfair assessment."

"Okay," said Lee, "but I have known Christians who left their faith for humanism. How do you explain that? I think they came to their senses. They studied the world for themselves and recognized that religion, even their Christian faith, doesn't explain the world sufficiently.

"I can introduce you to some of those people in our Humanist Club. They came to college as Christians, churchgoers, followers of Jesus, and now they have left that for the principles of humanism."

"I understand what you're saying. And it's a terrible thing when people leave Christ. But the human heart is complicated. You make it sound like they walked away from their faith because they suddenly came to the truth. I say they left the Truth.

"Look, there are people who go to church just to avoid repentance. Yah, that sounds strange but it's true. They may not even be conscious of what they're doing, but they think they're okay with God because they go to church. They confess that Jesus is their Lord, but deep inside they want their own way. Deep down they've never really come to grips with their sin and pride. Church becomes a kind of cover where they feel safe because they believe they please God, with the result that they actually avoid repenting of their rebelliousness inside.

"Life then has a way of exposing the charade to them and they walk away from Christ. Sometimes they are led away by humanistic arguments. Sometimes by other religions. Sometimes it's just the world and its pleasures that lead them away. Sometimes their rebellion comes out on their deathbed. But in all these cases, the reality is they never truly repented of their own way. Jesus was never truly their Lord.

"That's how deceitful the human heart can be. Yet their rejection of the Christian faith doesn't negate the true faith and repentance of others. Many have humbled themselves before God, turned from their own way, and humbly trusted Jesus as their Lord and Savior. God has changed them by His grace, and they know it. They are grateful and willing to serve the Lord no matter what. Such people will not walk away from Christ but will persevere in faith even if it costs them their life."

BLAME GAME

Lee paused; a bit taken back by the impact of that last thought. Then he replied, "Whatever you say about people's faith, the fact is, religion has been a source of division in the world. It fails to help society solve problems. It always ends up forcing certain rules, taking people's money, and then telling them what to believe. It's been a source of countless wars, and it still engenders divisions today!"

"**Do you mean to tell me that humanism doesn't do that? Tell me that the 20th century hasn't revealed numerous humanist leaders whose governments led to the deaths of millions and millions more people than religion ever has? Tell me that your humanism doesn't lead to rules, to taxes, to telling people what's acceptable to believe, or to division? Has it ever occurred to you that it's sin that causes problems, even for Christians?**"

"Whatever the cause," said Lee, "religion is so exclusivist. Why your God and not another? Why only Jesus?

"Don't you see, humanists affirm all people rather than deny some, we seek the evolutionary possibilities that make life better for everyone. Ours is a thought life that anyone can enjoy.

"We must admit that some humanists have failed in those goals and have become totalitarian and brutal. They lost sight of the goals. So, they failed to end the problems of poverty and lack of opportunity. Instead, their leaders ended up focusing on power and personal glory."

"**I'm glad to hear you admit that. Not many will. Many humanists gladly associate with totalitarian leaders and see them as heroes. Perhaps they do so only to oppose religions like Christianity. Or perhaps they admire the power such leaders project.**"

"Christians had their chance," said Lee. "The Church failed when it ran society."

"**Okay, and the Church admitted it. It's been hundreds of years since the Church ran the State. Christianity corrected that error. Now Christians see Church and State as separate but interdependent.**"

"How do you mean, interdependent?" asked Lee. "You Christians want a theocracy. You want everyone to be governed by the Bible and by your beliefs."

"**No, that's not how it works. Interdependence means that the Church needs the State for what God instituted the State for, and the State needs the Church for what God instituted the Church for.**

"**For example, the State creates laws to protect people's lives, liberty,** and property. The State is equipped to provide societal supports for economics, opportunity, security, and more.

"The Church is suited to teach people how to be moral, how to love God and others. God's laws govern the individual in a very personal way, between God and the individual. As a person is governed by God, he or she becomes a better member of society.

"The State needs people to be moral in order to create laws that are truly just. Christians teach a theocracy in a person's heart, not an institutional theocracy. True faith and repentance and true love for God are personal. They cannot be forced on someone. As a person gets right with God, as he or she encounters that change of heart that teaches one to love God and others, then everyone in society benefits."

"Humanism," said Lee, "also affects people's hearts, but not by focusing on a god, just on others and on society as a whole. That's why it can better affect all people. It leaves out the debates about God."

"You only exchange the debate about God for debates about people. You only exchange debates, you don't remove them. You argue about which philosopher or leader to aspire to, which idea to aspire to. That leaves you as acting like God over the people. Certain people or ideas become the a-theocracy. That's not what Christianity teaches.

"Christianity reveals a great and loving God whom people can come to know. He made them, provides for their life, and yet He also holds them accountable for their behavior. God has every right to do that. Learning to know Him and follow Him is far more exciting and satisfying than following people!"

"That all sounds great," said Lee. "But it's unproven. You can't prove to me it is true or that it works for all people."

"So, the millions of people who have found peace and help in Christ are not good evidence of Christianity? Christians are the ones who have championed helping the poor. Christians are the ones who teach being the Good Samaritan and helping your neighbor in need regardless of their race, color, or creed. Christianity teaches it is better to give than to receive, that it's a sin to covet or be greedy or to ignore the economic deprivations of others.

"You humanists are too busy debating your next great plan to save humanity, while for thousands of years Christians have been doing the difficult work of real change.

"Aren't you making religion a scapegoat for the failure of humanism? You humanists are on a treadmill that leads nowhere and merely repeats the past over and over again!"

"Whatever happened in the past is past," responded Lee. "Today we have greater advances in science and technology to help us. We understand the environment better and can better take care of people's needs. These things have the potential to improve life for all without the need for God.

"It's a different world now. We understand ourselves and our world better. Humanism has led the way to a better world, and science has been our savior."

"Aren't you claiming credit where you don't deserve it? I grant that many non-Christians have accomplished great things for people. But Christians have and still do contribute to science and technology, and to human betterment. Christians love God's world and see His hand in the laws that govern it. To uncover and understand the laws of nature is an exciting way to learn something about nature's Creator.

"Christians are naturally interested in science and technology as glimpses into God's great mind, wisdom, beauty, and power. And Christians fully understand that God-given human ability is to be used not only for God's glory but also for human good.

"It's just that Christians don't make an idol out of science. Science is not their 'god.' Anything that helps a person see God more clearly is a blessing. But God comes first."

PARTICULARS

Lee spoke up and said, "The humanist's goal is to achieve a set of principles that are useful for all people and lead to a better prospect for survival. Religion is too particular, too dogmatic, and too bounded by rituals and traditions. Most people feel they don't need all that to live a meaningful and productive life, or to help preserve the human species.

"Also, earlier you spoke about faith being necessary for understanding things. If faith, why your faith or why Christian particulars? I'm still not convinced that any faith is necessary if I can see something with my own eyes."

"Faith looks outside of self to know the reality and truth of something. Faith is therefore humbling. Faith in God makes a person God-centered in their thinking and that honors God and it humbles the believer. In essence, faith demonstrates the truly dependent place human beings are in before God.

"You said before that you can only accept the objective. There's nothing more objective, more real than God. Faith in God, therefore, connects one to the very source and meaning of life.

"Faith in God draws a person closer to their Maker and thus also draws their Maker closer to them. Faith is necessary for salvation because a person is not commended to God by their sins! Nor can they earn it by their supposed 'good deeds.' Each person must draw close to God by faith to get to know Him and to receive from Him His salvation.

"Christian Faith is unique in that God Himself accomplishes what is required to save a person. All they must do is believe and receive as a gift what God did. Again, one receives that gift by faith alone because nothing a sinner can do will commend them as deserving of salvation."

"Other religions have other ideas about salvation," said Lee. "I don't see why Jesus is really any different."

"Other religions focus on what people do for God, not on what God did for them.

"But let's talk about man for a moment. And I mean man anthropologically, not in terms of gender. Humanism is strictly man-centered. You have been enthusiastically defending that man-centered viewpoint of humanism. But what if I were to tell you that Christianity was man-centered long before secular humanism? Let me explain.

"Christianity goes back to the beginning of man to find its roots of humanism. God made men and women in His own image. Right then, at creation, man has been elevated to heights far above the animals. There is instantly a dignity and respect due to all people, regardless of who they are or what they believe, just for being humans made in God's image.

"Furthermore, loving one's fellow man is also part of Christian history and teaching. The roots of that also go back to the beginning because it's a part of how God made people. Such love for one another is embodied in God's image in man because it's embodied in God's Law, which reflects God's own character.

"My point is that you are arguing for universal humanistic claims when all along Christianity has made such claims while adding God as the ultimate reference point. The difference is that the Christian's focus on man is always subordinate to God. Christians see man as a product of God's hand. Therefore God-centeredness is primary, and man follows.

"What that means is that God is a common and fundamental reference point for *all people*. His revelation of humans made in His image is also a common and fundamental reference point. What you are trying to do is create your own common and fundamental reference point, that's all."

"So?" replied Lee. "What's wrong with that? If humanists can find a common and fundamental reference point in evolution and science, then what of it? If it works to make life better, then why knock it?"

"What you are trying to do is itself illogical. Let me explain. The thing itself cannot define itself. If a fish suddenly appeared in a fishbowl, would it make any sense for that fish to define itself? Wouldn't it make more sense for the fish to be told who and what it is by the one who knows, the one outside the fishbowl who put the fish there?

"All I'm saying is that a moving frame of reference cannot be fundamental, even if it is common. God is the only unmovable fundamental reference that can actually reveal who men are. If you argue evolution from physical matter as your fundamental reference point, your immoveable "god," so to speak, then evolution only speaks *through you* as *you* make conclusions and inferences. Once again, *you* become God, not matter or evolution. Any way you look at it, humanism always ends up pointing people back in upon themselves — that cannot be a valid way to know who you are."

"You forget," said Lee, "science is always there to help us understand, to clarify things. You ignore the vast fields of human study that help us understand ourselves and human behavior. You ignore all that science has investigated and concluded."

"Not true. The scientific method is limited to the physical. Science is great at making observations and drawing conclusions. And it has certainly done so with human behavior. But it is too limited to be an infallible method when dealing with the metaphysical or with that which it cannot observe or discover on its own.

"Right and wrong are not strictly a physical or chemical construct. I've talked about this before. Mere chemical reactions become meaningless as guides to right and wrong. Pure secular humanism ends up with varied opinions and a subsequent battle of wills to decide whose view dominates. That's hardly what I'd call a stationary fundamental reference point."

"So, again," said Lee sarcastically, "you want us to follow *your* God?"

"You make it sound so crass. Think of it this way, God wants *you* to follow *Him*. In fact, that's why He created you the way you are, different from the animals. He loves you and wants you to love Him. His heart is so great that He even went to amazing lengths to bring you to Himself and provide a way of reconciliation.

"Don't see His love as restrictive or oppressive, but as winsome and desirous of what's best for you. Again, as I said before, when a person grasps the love of God through Jesus Christ, he or she wants to know God and love God as a response to God's grace shown to them. Christianity is about a relationship with God first, then others; it's not just about rules and rituals."

"But Christianity seems so disunited," responded Lee. "It's so hard to look at all the different denominations and theological creeds and make sense of it. At least humanism has some well-defined principles."

"Your point is well taken but is not exactly correct. Humanism is also diverse with numerous sects vying for their own positions. Also, there are well founded fundamentals in Christianity that all Christians believe. For example, the Apostles Creed."

"But," replied Lee, "now you're focusing on your particulars again. Where's the liberty in that?"

"So, are you suggesting that humanists don't have their particulars?"

"No," said Lee, "of course we do. It's just that I want to decide for myself if it's true or not."

"Now, let's get something straight. I hope we can both agree that people must choose. When the State or the Church *forces* people to think a certain way then thought-oppression results and true freedom is lost. I think we can agree that some humanists and some Christians have been guilty of doing that.

"Christians believe in liberty of conscience and freedom of choice. Change must come as each person, on their own, comes to faith and understanding of God through Jesus Christ.

"You affirm your faith and understanding in evolution and science. But hopefully, you also affirm freedom of choice?"

"Of course I do," said Lee. "But I choose secular particulars over Christian ones."

"Got it."

DIFFERENT STANDARDS

"Look, this is how I see it," said Lee, "you Christians have your minds in the clouds. This world needs our attention. People are the focus of humanism. If your God helps you help people, then fine. Otherwise your religion is a distraction from life's most pressing needs.

"That's how I see the world. To me, the idea of God becomes an unnecessary distraction from people who need me. I don't need God to help me or 'show me the way,' so to speak."

"There's nothing wrong with focusing on people. Christians do that in many ways. It's great that you see the importance of people, but you miss how God sees people.

"God doesn't see as humans see; He sees far more. He judges hearts and motives. He judges character. He knows a person's inmost and unspoken thoughts. He reads the truth about a person's heart.

"There is more going on here than meets the eye."

"There's the rub," replied Lee. "I only care about what meets my eyes or ears or hands. Everything else is a judgment call of someone else. And why should I listen to them?"

"Is jealousy or envy a judgment call? Is pride? Is anger? Is lust or greed? You judge yourself by yourself. How can that be a standard for truth?

"God judges people by Himself. That's what makes His judgments true."

"Why should I recognize a standard I don't see?" asked Lee.

"We do seem to be running in circles here a little, but let me try to express it all another way.

"Because humans are made in God's images, they are accountable to God's standards. He has revealed His standards in the Bible. Now, I know you deny that, but I'm saying you are made in God's image and accountable to His standards no matter what you think. You cannot deny who you are by God's creation.

"People want to redefine themselves, their identity, their gender, their nature. But it's not possible. That's like a cat denying its cat-ness or a horse denying its horse-ness.

"God defines who people are and that cannot be changed or denied. Trying to deny it is both futile and fraught with trouble.

"So, to deny God's standard is to deny yourself. Try as you might, your efforts will only end in disappointment."

"Truth and identity are mine to discover," said Lee. "My life is a journey that I choose. My standard is mine, and I adjust to and live with other people's standards just fine as long as I'm causing no harm to them and they're causing no harm to me."

"What is harm? The greatest harm you do to yourself and others is to reject God and His standards. Yes, you feel like a king or a master of your own destiny, but that's a lie.

"I'm telling you that God will hold every human being accountable to His standard, not to their own or to anyone else's.

"Don't you see that your Creator has every right to do that? Don't you see the pride in your attitude? People must walk humbly before God and seek Him and look for what He requires of them."

"That seem so arbitrary," said Lee. "Who knows what He wants?"

"Are you looking for a personal invitation from God Himself? Read the Bible. There God invites all to come to Him, freely, without cost, and receive His mercy and grace.

"Those who humbly trust Him He will lead and show the way. That kind of trust is not blind; it centers upon God as He is revealed in the Bible. He personally guides those who love and trust Him and seek Him with all their heart."

Lee was silent for a moment, unsure how to respond since he knew that Christians treat the Bible as God's word. To challenge that would only result in repeating areas they'd already covered.

"God looks at the heart. He sees things people don't because their sin blinds them to His standard and to the error of their way.

"Because God's judgments are not executed immediately, people feel no urgency to change. But that's a lying disposition. Don't trust your feelings but trust that God will be faithful to what He says."

Lee still said nothing. He recognized that his own standard and the standards of others were arbitrary. But he was unwilling to concede any ground. He still wanted to believe his position had to be right.

"Look, you can't judge God by your standards. You must take Him at His word. Anything less than that makes God less than God. I cannot convince you to look to Him, but I appeal to you to do so.

"When it comes to trusting God, what you don't know — or don't believe — can hurt you. No one will be able to justify themselves before God by their own standards."

"Then what hope has anyone?" asked Lee. "You seem to promote something that's unattainable. God holds people to a standard they can't keep?"

"Yes, and that's where His grace comes in so wonderfully. God gives to sinners *not* what they deserve, but what they *don't* deserve.

"God loves people so much that He accomplished through His Son Jesus all they need for salvation. To humble one's self and trust God in Jesus' name is all that's required to receive this grace."

KNOWING GOD

Lee felt a little moved by the idea that God loved him. But he still had questions spinning about in his mind. So, he asked, "You Christians speak about knowing God, but how can you know someone you can't see? That's why I think prayer is just a catharsis. In fact, religion itself is just a kind of emotional release. It helps people cope with fear, like the fear of the future or the unknown.

"But I feel I can face the present rationally and deal with my fears that way. A catharsis for me is just knowing more about the causes and effects of nature. As I learn more, I feel better. So, I don't see a need for God."

"First, I agree with you in the sense that every human being has his or her own cathartic method. Some deal with fears by pursuing pleasure or money, others art, or like you, by science and philosophy. And so, I agree that religion can also become just a catharsis, but it isn't always that way. The point being that all people seek to deal with fears of the future and the unknown.

"That's where faith comes in. Again, faith is believing something is true even when you don't know all the details. Faith is having confidence in something or someone to help you through those fears.

"For you, your faith clings to science to help you deal with life. You say others cling to religion. But my point is that everyone looks to something or someone for a kind of catharsis, as you call it.

"Second, knowing God is something that satisfies the soul in a most wonderful way. It's not a catharsis. Knowing God has both a firm root in reason and a strong hold on faith. Knowing God speaks deeply to the human spirit because God created humans in His own image. There is, therefore, nothing in nature quite like knowing God. Knowing God combines faith and reason with the deepest possible satisfaction of the soul.

"Third, knowing God is relational. You cannot have a personal relationship with nature, at least not one that speaks to you as a person, or to your human nature.

"It's like this. You may have a relationship with your pet dog, but it's limited. You may love hiking in the wild, communing with nature so to speak, but it only touches certain emotions in you. Neither a pet nor nature itself can relate to you like another human being.

"Now imagine a person who not only can relate to your human nature, but to everything about you. Imagine one who knows every detail of your life, every thought before you speak it, every need, every fear, every doubt, every hope. That's God!

"God is the only person who truly knows you. And He is knowable by you. So, unlike any other relationship you can have, knowing God is unique and special."

"But how do I relate to one I don't see?" asked Lee. "I mean, how does God speak to me? What words does He use since I don't hear Him or see Him?"

"Those are excellent questions. Of course, I spoke before about how God reveals Himself. I mentioned creation, the Bible, and His Son, Jesus Christ. But since you're asked about words, then God speaks to you through the Bible. His word is there in the Bible, which is one reason Christians insist that the Bible be called 'God's word.' The Bible is God-breathed, as I said before, which establishes it as God's word.

"Yet, there's something even more profound about Jesus that you must understand. The Bible calls Jesus, 'The Word'! He is God's word become flesh. He is God — the Person of the Son — become man to speak directly to people and to reveal God's love directly to them. That's both exciting and profound.

"So, reading the Bible becomes more than just filling your head with information. It becomes a personal interaction with God Himself in a manner which engages both your reason and your faith. It becomes a personal encounter with God that leads to a relationship that directly impacts your human nature."

"Well," said Lee, "that certainly is more than I even considered, I'll admit that. That's a perspective I've never thought about before.

"So, you're saying that the Bible is how God speaks to a person and a person speaks to God?"

"Yes, almost. The Bible is the basis for all speaking to God. Of course, anyone at any time can simply pray to God. But God will hear and respond in accordance with His word, the Bible. That's why it is so central to knowing God."

"I see," said Lee, thinking out loud. "Knowing God would be a fascinating thing. I just still struggle with how to relate it to science."

"Look, many people, even philosophers, get hung up by the limits of science and the scientific method. But knowing God doesn't contradict science, it just goes into areas that you can't discover on your own., Knowing God comes through God's personal revelation of Himself. It's not by scientific discovery as if one could find God by searching under a rock, or something like that.

"Rather, you come to know Him by His own revelation of Himself. Isn't that just how you come to know any person? Don't you get to know people as they tell you about themselves?"

"Yes," said Lee. "Yes, I do," he said with a little smile.

RADICAL HUMANISM

Lee went home feeling a little perplexed. He was starting to feel somewhat torn between his humanism and Christianity. Some of the barriers he had about Christianity had been taken down. And some weaknesses in humanism had become apparent. He felt a little unsure of himself. That night, he attended a student Humanist Club meeting.

At the meeting, the subject of religion came up. A student began to express his thoughts on the dangers of organized religion.

"Organized religion," said the student, "is just a form of escape from reality. It creates codependency, fears of eternal damnation, unscientific myths, and unseen gods who supposedly affect things.

"Organized religion is, therefore, a danger to humanity and must be neutralized. To do that we need to win the minds of youth through education. And we must win control of governments. Then, once we are the dominant societal influence, we can marginalize organized religions and make them relics of the past!"

The others listened. But some, having never learned how to enter into the worldview of others, blithely agreed. Others were more hesitant.

Lee, however, didn't say anything at first because the scene weighed heavy upon his mind. He pondered the matter, then spoke.

"What if there really is a God who has revealed Himself and we're just missing it all?" asked Lee. "What if the Bible is true and God did do all those things it says? We can't disprove them. We only say they are untrue because we don't observe them now."

"Lee," said the student, "what are you saying? This doesn't sound like you at all. What have you been reading? Are you going to church or something?"

"No," said Lee, with a grin. "But I've met a Christian and we've been having a lot of discussions about Christianity and humanism. A lot of what the Christian says makes sense. I don't believe it, but I can see why others do.

"What scares me about your comments about organized religion is that you set yourself up as judge. You set your opinions above others. Why can't we just accept that others believe differently? If we argue science will one day vindicate us, then why can't we wait? You know they claim that science will one day vindicate them, and maybe it will."

"Lee," said the student, "you've got to stop talking to these people. You know they're wrong. They just want to get you in their church and take your money."

Chuckles came from the group.

"No," replied Lee, "that's what we think. But that's not what they're trying to do. They care about our souls. They don't reject the here and now, but they care enough about the future that they point us to God. That's what this person wants, and I've not encountered religion like this before."

"Well," said the student, "encounter this. Life is full of relativistic thinking and situations. It's not about Absolutes, except the Absolute of that statement! It all boils down to behavior. Do we want the freedom to do what we want with our bodies, or do we want some god to tell us what to do?"

"But," said Lee, "what if knowing God is really a beautiful thing? What if His rules are intended not to restrict us but to allow us to be truly free within the boundaries of those rules?"

"Lee," said the student, "I think you're tired and confused. You need a vacation, man!"

TRUTH AND CULTURE

One of Lee's friends, a philosophy student, spoke up. "Lee," he said, "how can you be drawn into Christianity? You know that it is just a cultural construct of a people who lived two thousand years ago. Westerners have taken what was a simple faith and complicated it with institutional and Western thought and bias."

Lee responded, "They would argue that they are standing on the Bible."

"But," replied the philosophy student, "that means they are imposing their own opinions and making them absolutes. How can we accept that kind of dogmatism? Words have a personal construct as we read them. My construct is just as valid as theirs!"

Lee nodded in agreement. But then he added, "Aren't we advocating a kind of absolute too? Aren't we also being dogmatic?"

The meeting ended and the students went home.

The next day Lee passed by that familiar bench again and found the Christian sitting there. He decided to present the idea that words have meaning only as people individually interpret them.

"Hi!" said Lee.

"Hi!"

"Nice to bump into you," said Lee. "I have a question to ask you."

"Ask away!"

"How can you Christians take your faith from the Bible when words we read are subject to the constructs of meaning we put on them?"

"First, you wouldn't bother asking me that question if you didn't think I would interpret it a certain way. Second, it's true that there are some things in the Bible that are difficult to understand, but the vast majority of it is clear and can be read with comprehension by children.

"You are reflecting upon a Postmodern idea that words have no ultimate meaning and truth is only true when considered from the perspective of the individual, such that any idea can be truth.

"Such philosophy is ultimately absurd to me. It strikes me as an intellectual trick used by some to justify their own opinions and deflect responsibility for the consequences for what they believe."

"Aren't words conditioned by culture?" asked Lee. "Isn't Christianity a product of its time?

"You say you hold to absolutes from the Bible, but even the Bible was written in an ancient cultural context. Things have long since changed. We live in a vastly different context now. So won't that change the Bible's relevancy?"

"Cultures may change, but the human heart doesn't. The same ideas and issues people struggle with today were struggled with thousands of years ago. To put a different outfit on a person doesn't change the person. Technology and other cultural changes are like a new set of cloths, but the person underneath hasn't changed."

"Are you saying that humans haven't advanced since ancient times?" asked Lee.

"In a sense, yes. Certainly knowledge and experience has changed. Learning and medicine and science have advanced greatly. People today are living in unprecedented times.

"Yet, there are still issues of truth, of life, of meaning, of origin, of destiny, of morality, of ethics, and so on that are truly the same. It's as though you could take a man or woman who lived five thousand years ago, plop them down in society today, and they would become just like anyone else. They would adjust to the new culture and yet struggle with the same issues of life that they did in their former culture.

"My concern with your position is that it gives justification for creating your own standards and imposing them on others."

"What do you mean?" asked Lee. "How am I creating new standards when I interpret things my own way?"

"People will always try to justify their views. People will create their own moral laws, laws that substantiate their view of life, and then try to impose them on others."

"So what?" replied Lee. "You just want to impose the Bible on others!"

"No, that's not true. Christians argue that the Bible is God's revealed Truth, it reveals God's law and grace. Yet, the Bible also teaches that each person should love and trust God, and in that spirit follow what God says. We cannot *make* a person love and trust God. That's why salvation is not a corporate matter but an individual one. Each person is confronted with the Truth and must respond to it."

Lee replied, "But history is filled with examples of Christians imposing their laws on others."

"Wait a minute. Don't you think every culture does that? You make it sound as if Christians are the only ones who ever did that.

"Here's how Christian teaching *should* affect culture. As the people change by knowing Jesus, so will their culture and laws. That's not imposing Christianity, that's freedom of conscience and democracy at work."

"But what if I don't agree with your Christian laws?" asked Lee.

"What if Christians don't agree with your secular laws?"

Lee got the point. Feeling a bit weary of the discussion he waved and walked away.

Soon he ran into his philosophy friend. Lee asked him, "If Christianity is just a cultural construct and our views are too, then why do we care whose views dominate?"

"We don't live in the ancient Middle East, Lee," replied the friend.

"I know," said Lee, "but if Christian beliefs work for some people today, then why oppose them?"

"We oppose them," said the friend, "because they oppose us! Their views oppose our views of free and open thought."

"No. That's not true," said Lee. "Christians believe people need to make choices, they don't believe that loving and trusting God can be forced on someone. They also believe that people must take responsibility for the consequences of their ideas. That seems reasonable to me."

The two then separated, content to solve these issues another day.

CHURCH

The following Sunday Lee found himself walking the downtown streets of his college town and thinking. He then found himself outside a local church, where he saw people entering. He thought to himself, "Why not go in and just hear what the preacher says? It will probably be irrational or crazy stuff, but then I'll know." So, he entered and sat down in the back.

The people prayed and sang, while he quietly observed. Then the preacher got up to speak. His message was entitled, "God's Fatherly Heart." He spoke from Luke 15.

"One familiar expression of God's fatherly heart is found in Jesus' parable of the Prodigal Son," began the preacher. "You know the story.

"A rebellious son demands his inheritance while his father lives. His father gives it to him. He then squanders it all on wild living.

"Now poor and destitute, the son returns to his father sorrowful and repentant. And the father joyfully forgives and receives him.

"But there's also an older son. He is rebellious in his own way. He is proud and self-righteous. He becomes angry as the father blesses the returning son. But his father also reaches out to him.

"You see, the father in the parable represents God, our Heavenly Father. The sons represent us. We are lost and rebellious, prideful and selfish, in different ways. Some are given to wild living; some to a self-righteous life. Yet, we are all lost, wandering sinners in need of the Father's forgiveness and love.

"When we come to our senses — like the prodigal son did — we see how tiring our pride and sin have become. We want the peace and rest that comes from knowing the love of God's fatherly heart.

"What does this parable reveal to us about God's heart? Let me mention several things.

"First, God's heart is patient with sinners. When the younger son demanded his share of the inheritance, his father complied. God too gives to all life, kindness, and provisions. He lets us enjoy the fruits of His world. He gives us talents and abilities. God patiently gives while we take. Why? Why do we just take? It's because we have the same spirit seen in the younger son.

"The Bible says of God in Romans 2:4, 'Or do you despise the riches of his kindness, restraint, and patience, not recognizing that God's kindness is intended to lead you to repentance?' We see that heart of kindness, restraint, and patience in the father's heart. No doubt that love kept gnawing at the younger son's heart and mind while he was astray. And it reveals God's patience, giving us time to repent.

"Second, God's heart is lovingly longing for sinners to return to Him. We see this in how the father saw his son while still a long way off. This was not a chance glance. The father was longing for his son's return and looking for it.

"God's longing is expressed in the words of Hosea 14:2, 'Take words of repentance with you and return to the LORD ... I will heal their apostasy; I will freely love them, for my anger will have turned from him.' God longs for *you* to take words with you and return to Him!

"Third, God's heart is forgiving. When the wayward son returns, the first words out of the father were, 'Quick, bring out the best robe and put it on him; put a ring on his finger and sandals on his feet.' This is a picture of full and free forgiveness.

"The robe reminds us that God covers our sins and shame with the atoning sacrifice of His Son and then with His own righteousness like a robe.

"The ring reminds us that we are reinstated into God's family and share anew His inheritance.

"The sandals remind us that we are no longer slaves of sin, wandering lost, but have returned home to the father's loving care. Our feet are home again!

"Fourth, God's heart is compassionate. Before he even spoke to his returning son, the father embraced him and kissed him. This reveals the deep compassion of God. Many people falsely charge God with wrong, but God is good and compassionate and gracious.

"Fifth, God's heart is joyful. How justified the father would have been to punish his son. Instead, he celebrates! He killed the fattened calf – reserved for special occasions – to celebrate his son's return.

"That return was big. And it's big when anyone returns to the Lord. In fact, Jesus said in verse 10, 'I tell you, in the same way, there is joy in the presence of God's angels over one sinner who repents.' The angels may rejoice, but they are just following God's lead!

"Sixth, God's heart is winsome. God is not trying to push people away; He's inviting us to return to Him. That's why the gospel is the 'good news;' it's God's invitation to salvation.

"We see God's winsomeness in how the father treats the younger son, and in how he treats the older son too. The older son is bitter and resentful of the father's goodness to the repentant son.

"If the younger son was a slave to his passions, the older son was a slave to his pride. But the father goes out and pleads with the older son, trying to draw him in again.

"In the parable we see the heart of God on display. It's also the heart of Jesus, God's Son. Have you returned to God the Father through Jesus the Son? Why not? A more sincere and winsome invitation you will not find than God's invitation to full and free forgiveness and restoration to an inheritance with Him in glory."

The service ended and Lee walked out, careful to avoid contact with anyone. For he felt awkward there. Yet, at the same time, he was drawn to what the preacher said. He had not thought of God in those personal terms before. He could see what the strange person had said to him about how God wants a relationship with people.

A FATHER'S LOVE

As Lee returned home from the church service, he passed the bench he often sat on to speak with the stranger. He sat down and began to ask himself some questions.

"I wonder if this idea of a relationship with God is real? How fascinating would it be to know God? But how can it be? Isn't what we know subject to scientific investigation? But the Christian said it is faith and reason that we need. It's not one versus the other; it's both. So, can I believe and know God? Would that be scientific?"

Lee looked up and the stranger stood there before him and said, **"Good afternoon!"**

"Hi!" said Lee, with a bit of a surprised look on his face.

The stranger sat down.

"I saw you in church today."

"How's that?" asked Lee.

"Are you drawn to the love of such a father as in the parable of the Prodigal Son?"

"Yes," said Lee. "I never heard of God portrayed like that before. I see how people can be drawn in by God's love."

"He loves you; He loves everyone. Yet, He is also a judge. He is just and holy. But many people stop there and assume that's all He is to them, a just judge, so they stay away from Him. They figure, 'If I get close, since I'm a sinner and He is holy and just, then He'll only condemn me.'"

"But," said Lee, "He's not like that, is He? He is patient, longing, forgiving, compassionate, joyful, and winsome."

"Someone's been listening at church! That's great. Yes, people need to keep God's love in mind because apart from that love, they really have no hope.

"Humanists get very excited about their vision for humanity. But they neglect God's love as though it's irrelevant. They think they can muster up a form of ethics and culture and economics without God that will work for all people and not end up empty. It won't happen.

"The highest goal anyone can have is to know, love, and serve God. Far from being a distraction from human service, it's a great motivator.

"Did you know that when God's Son took on flesh and was born a man, He came as a humble servant? He did not come at this first coming as a reigning King or Lord, but as a meek servant. He showed people

what God truly expects of all human beings — a humble servant's heart toward God and others."

"You know," said Lee, "my father left my mother when I was a boy."

"I'm sorry to hear that."

"I was bitter for many years," said Lee. "Then, I concluded that we all make choices and that was just his. I figured my mother and I could survive on our own. We didn't need him."

"Sometimes people project onto God the image of their own father. When their earthly father failed them or was unfaithful or abusive, they assumed God must be like that. But it's not fair to project such images on God. Rather, He must be understood as He reveals Himself, like in the parable of the Prodigal Son."

"Yes," said Lee, "I agree. A Christian has every right to draw conclusions about God from the book they claim is God's word.

"I think that many people don't know your God at all. They have their own ideas about Him, right or wrong."

"That's very perceptive. So, how do people come to know God rightly, you might ask? The answer is through His word, the Bible. And specifically, through the revelation of His Son, Jesus. To know Jesus is to know God. To have the Son is to have the Father too. And, to have the Father and the Son is to have the Holy Spirit. If you truly have one, you have them all."

"Now," asked Lee, "are you saying God has three parts — Father, Son, and Holy Spirit?"

"No, God is one God existing in three Persons and each Person is fully God."

Lee asked, "How can you expect people to understand that? It makes no sense. How can God be one and three at the same time?"

"You cannot impose your scientific method on the transcendence of God. The God who made all things is greater than the things He made. You see the world in fixed dimensions, scientifically, yet God exists in a far greater dimension. He who made the universe is infinite. The vastness of His Being is incomprehensible to any creature.

"Therefore, you must understand God on God's terms. He is one God in three Persons. Think of it like this. God is never lonely or bored. He exists in perfect bliss with Himself, yet He chose to create. No doubt, He felt joy in revealing Himself to the lesser beings He made. He felt delight in revealing to them His love and kindness, grace, truth, faithfulness, and such. He takes no pleasure in their destruction, but He delights in them coming to know Him."

"So," said Lee, "if every Person of God is God, then you're saying Jesus, too, was God. You're saying He was not human?"

"No, Jesus was fully man. He was fully human, yet fully God and divine as well. Consider how that fact impacts your view of humanism. Don't the divine and human natures of Jesus Christ make Christian humanism a much greater concept than that of secular humanism?

"That God took on human flesh makes the Christian view of mankind that much more elevated. God loves people. So much so that when it was necessary, He came to them, born of a woman, grew from childhood, and did for them what they could not do for themselves."

"What do you mean?" asked Lee. "How did God do for us what we cannot do for ourselves?"

"God accomplished the full and free salvation that sinners need. People could never pay back to God the debt they owed from the guilt of their sins. Yet, Jesus took God's wrath on Himself for them when He died on the cross. By trusting Jesus as Savior, that death becomes a covering for the guilt and penalty of the individual's sins. It's called an atonement.

"The Father God allowed His Son to die on a cross as a substitute for sinners so that they can return to Him and be forgiven. God accounts the debt the sinner owes Him to be satisfied by His Son's death. He paid it and the repentant sinner won't have to. That, too, is great love.

"Think of it; God so loved people that He took on flesh, bore their sins, invites them to return to Him, and rejoices when they do. That's how much God loves human beings."

RESCUE MISSION – DAY ONE

Somehow, Lee's friends at the Humanist Club found out that he went to church and determined to do something about it. They knew there was a humanist conference coming to a nearby college. So, they devised a plan to get Lee there, to rescue him from his vain curiosity into Christianity.

Lee agreed to go.

At the conference, a gentleman began by outlining the humanistic view of life and how it relates to various aspects of human experience.

"It's a privilege to be with you at this conference," began the speaker. "I know that it's sometimes helpful to be re-grounded in the principles that make us humanists. So, let me outline for you some of those basic principles as they relate to the areas of religion, ethics, personhood, and culture.

"Religious beliefs purport to elevate a person to 'spiritual' experiences. We don't deny the validity of an experience, but we know that such experiences are purely psychological. We deny that the experience has a higher meaning that points to God.

"What's more, the dogmatic parts of religions cannot be joined with science. They are incompatible. We cannot join the subjective and the objective. Religion as a feeling is one thing, but as a genuine guide to reality, it is something else. We must rely upon the principles of scientific investigation to ground ourselves.

"I have also seen that attempts to redefine dogmatic religions inevitably fail. Therefore, such religions cannot be the basis for human advancement. I'm confident they will eventually fade away from culture as science removes all superstition and demonstrates their irrelevance.

"Ethical areas have been fertile ground for criticism against secular humanism. But, we form our basis for ethics from culture and experience. We say that ethics flow out of the human experience and are not dictated to us by some outside being. They are, therefore, purely situational and engage a moment in history.

"We humans are capable of reasoning our way through situations that call for value judgments. No one has an exclusive hold on the wisdom required to make such ethical choices. Humankind has all it needs to survive ethically in the modern world.

"Personhood is also central to humanism. The freedom of the mind, the will, and the emotions make the entire person free. Anything that limits human creativity and individuality should be avoided or held to as private opinions.

"Personal liberty of thought and choice extends to all areas of life, including sexuality. All consenting forms of sexual expression are valid. All expressions of gender that empower the individuality of a person are valid. We support the individual's right to end their life on their own terms. We support a woman's right over her body to have an abortion. And we reject all forms of enslavement of a person.

"We see culture as that from which we derive our motivation and determination. Culture changes because people change. Therefore, governments cannot be tied to fixed religious dogma. People must be free to evolve as they see fit.

"Therefore, all people should have a voice in government, so long as that voice doesn't hinder the broader good of society. To that end we proclaim the total separation of Church and State. Because of the subjective nature of religion, it cannot be used as a reasoning force for governance. We must rely upon the secular State as the only place where humans can determine their own destiny.

"We aim at creating societal structures, both governmental and economic, that seek the collective good of all rather than the benefits to a few. We aspire to a world without national boundaries where those benefits flow freely to any individual.

"People of every part of the world must work together to plan for our future. Global climate change and resource sustainability must be at the forefront of a world agenda for humanity to survive. This generation must act, or the next generation will suffer.

"To help achieve these goals, we rely on technology and good planning. Education is a key to success for meeting the requirements to sustain human life at a quality of life that all can enjoy.

"In conclusion, we cannot wait for dogmatic religions to change. We cannot wait for greedy capitalists to change. We cannot wait for traditionalists in government and society to change. We must act as the change agents for all.

"We are responsible for human survival. We cannot wait for others to reconcile with this agenda. We must move forward with what we know will work out in the end and benefit the human species the most."

Lee listened to it all. His friends encouraged him and rallied to his side. For the moment he felt reaffirmed in his humanist convictions.

RESCUE MISSION – DAY TWO

On the final day of the conference, another speaker gave a closing address.

She began, "As we trace the history of humanism, we find that humanist thinking has evolved to give us greater clarity and a more succinct way of understanding humanity. We appreciate the zeal and the goals of former generations, but we also acknowledge that sometimes they presented the principles of humanism in harsher terms.

"We aspire to affirm the consequences of our principles, but we must do so by first elevating the ideals. For, once those ideals are apparent, we are convinced people will naturally be drawn to them.

"We understand how the unknown can make people lean on deities or a higher power. We appreciate the struggle the human mind can go through. But, we offer a better way to a sense of peace and comfort about life.

"We offer people a way to face reality with satisfaction and enthusiasm. We offer them the joy of being, doing, and knowing for themselves without any restrictions.

"The key to this is science and education. We know that what we see and observe is real and tangible, and so it confronts us with the ultimate questions of life. Where do I come from? Who am I? Where am I going?

"Rather than look to a deity we cannot see, we seek to answer those questions by what we can see. That which we see, to us is knowable. Not that we claim to understand all mysteries, but we do claim that if something is real, it is knowable, and if knowable then we have all the tools necessary to know it.

"Where do I come from? Prior to Darwin, most of humanity assumed we came from the hand of a deity. Darwin showed us that there are processes in the universe that themselves give birth to life. Therefore, we are not afraid to say we are the products of evolution.

"Who am I? This question has also plagued humankind for millennia. We want to believe that we are spun from some divine consciousness, but we have no way to know how it happened. Different cultures have dreamt of different ways such divine beings made us. But we need look no further than ourselves.

"You are who you are! That's all. We humanists celebrate you for being you. We don't have to define you. You define you. Then, let us all encourage each other and affirm each other in your discovery of yourself!

"Where am I going? That question has led many to embrace a mythology of divine destiny and providence. To many, a god orders the world and moves it toward a certain goal. The deity promises life after death for obedience and faith. Yet, we see no evidence of such a goal or of such promises.

"Looking objectively at life, we must acknowledge death. But we do so with a growing appreciation for our individual consciousness and our potential contribution to the consciousness of others. In that frame of mind, we face death in the hope of benefiting others.

"This is modern humanism. Although some see it in strict political terms, it is not like that. Although some espouse it to justify violence, they should not. The consequences of misunderstanding and misapplying humanist principles have led to events those principles seek to avoid!

"Our words are those of peace and a sincere desire for all people everywhere to live life to its fullest, while helping others along the way."

At the end of her speech, she received a standing ovation.

REBUTTAL

Lee had settled back firmly into his humanist ideals. A few weeks later, he passed that bench where he had previously met the stranger. To his amazement, there stood the Christian.

"I thought you were long gone," said Lee. "I must say, I found our former discussions interesting, but I've settled back to my former convictions. You Christians don't have the ultimate answers to solve human problems. They must be solved collectively, and not by focusing on some deity we can't see or by reading some antiquated book.

"Someday you Christians will realize you are wrong. Science will set us all straight. The species will press forward successfully because of dedicated humanists, not Christians.

"Technology will make a better world for all. And, eventually, we'll have one world system that all can live freely and harmoniously in.

"You Christians put that all off to the future, but we say it can happen now!"

The Christian paused reflectively, concerned for Lee, and then began to speak gently, but firmly.

"The Bible says, rebellion is as the sin of witchcraft, and stubborn defiance is as the worst wickedness and idolatry. You set yourselves up as God, making judgments you have no right to make, and are blind to your exceeding self-importance. What's more, you promote rebellion toward God that can only lead to eternal suffering. You say you care about tomorrow, but only as tomorrow suites you today. You are blind to the eternal consequences of your beliefs. Therefore, I must try to help you see the error of your thinking.

"Regarding religion. What you miss is that all people have a fundamental God-given desire to worship. Unfortunately, they will usually worship themselves or others in some way. But God made human beings to worship Him alone. That's because He alone is truly worthy of worship. And He made humans to understand His creation, to study it, and enjoy it, not so that they will exalt themselves but so they worship Him.

"That spirit of worship generates what you think of as spirituality. It's the same spirit that makes you feel good when you affirm others who affirm you. You may not call that expression worship, but that's what it is! Yet you ignore the God who gave you life and consciousness.

"The highest form of emotion and motivation can come from worship, but only when it is rightly placed where it belongs — on God. The human soul is moved by many features of life — what is called art, science, music, culture, and so on. Beauty moves the human soul to a sense of awe. That's the worship I'm talking about. But such worship is wrongly placed when directed toward the creature rather than the Creator. Therefore, it becomes self-affirming rather than God honoring. It causes one to bow to self or others rather than God. That's rebellion!

"Regarding ethics. You create a system of right and wrong that merely affirms your will. You have no anchor points. And science cannot rescue you here. Right and wrong become a matter of opinion and choice.

"Yet, the greatest ethical standard is that which is true. And, that which is true conforms to the One who created human beings, and that's God. The Creator knows what's best for the creature. His standard is what conforms rightly to human nature. However, we don't see all people doing that standard because of sin. Sin is lawlessness and rebellion. Sin is stubbornness and defiance of God. Sin is therefore unethical and immoral. And the standard of judgment is not made by people but by God, the Judge. To set yourself up as Judge is rebellion and defiance before God.

"Regarding the person. Sadly, I must point out your error. You reject enslavement, yet you affirm abortion. How can that be? You see abortion as a choice for the mother, an autonomous choice, and you think science proves the fetus is not a person. So, you use personal autonomy and science as an authority — arguments that affirm your humanism — to make a terrible choice.

"Slave owners in the old American South argued for the rights of the owner over the slave. The owner was autonomous. And they formed elaborate arguments in support of slavery, even by twisting the Bible, to suggest that the slave was not a person. Thus, they used their supposed autonomy and coupled it with their supposed authority to enslave human beings, even kill them. Abortion does precisely the same thing. And it's all the fruit of thinking too highly of self, of ignoring God's will to do your own, and that's disobedience.

"Your understanding of the person is false. God created each person with a dignity that He established. You have no right to say suicide or euthanasia are okay when done on the person's own terms, or that abortion is a right. Nor do you have the right to define gender or sexuality, or institutions like marriage. You are playing God, and that's rebellion. You dishonor God and trample upon His sovereignty. How will He not be angry with you for ignoring His authority and imposing your own will?

"Regarding culture. I'm sure you think you're doing well by ignoring religion in State issues. But aren't you just elevating your own opinions to law? You ignore the most important document of law, the one written by the very finger of God — the Ten Commandments. Instead, you relegate that document to an ancient religion and so disqualify it and remove it from consideration. That's wrong.

"That law is the greatest and most relevant law to humans because it is God's law of love. The Ten Commandments affirm God's will for people to love Him and love each other. They form the basis for true liberty because they govern how people are to respect the life, freedom, and property of others. In fact, true justice is defined by keeping God's Law, not by accepting or conforming to the ideas or opinions of people.

"You think you can create justice and love without God — you can't! Your ideas of justice and love will always degenerate into the moment and be surpassed by a different generation. You remove the foundation of stone hoping to build a better one out of sand. It cannot last. Your efforts to build a perfect world without God will degenerate into chaos and wickedness, or, into an authoritarian world so strict and dogmatic that no one will be able to think for themselves. Freedom of thought will degenerate into only thinking the way you do. You will un-achieve what you claim to achieve. And, more importantly, God will not be with you.

"Regarding nations. You want one world order without remembering how God rebuked such a vision at the Tower of Babel. Nations were created by God to restrain evil. What's more, by reducing finite creatures to work within smaller groups, they have greater freedom to create ideas and traditions that others can learn from and that will affirm their identity. Sadly, people become proud of themselves and their achievements. They begin to feel superior. Then, they act like the devil himself and try to dominate others.

"God established nations so that evil can be restrained. Your vision, if fulfilled, will end up with Satan in charge of all of you. You'll all be his oppressed slaves. You'll only become confirmed and confined in your rebellion against God. Your last state will be far worse than your first! For, you'll never understand man's inhumanity to man until you understand that it's not due to economic or social injustices, or politics, but sin in the human heart.

"God is God. There is no other. He is very patient, gentle, and kind. He even shows His love to His enemies. Yet, you can push Him too far. He will hold people responsible for their actions. You claim such ideas to be fearmongering by threats of hell and damnation. Yet, you also in your own ways threaten those who disagree with you. The difference is your views have eternal consequences. So, the cost of your rebellion is staggering upon all who join you.

"Far from saving humankind, you codify its doom. You guarantee its slavery to people in power and to Satan. You fix as definitive the eternal destinies of millions. And all for what? For the satisfaction of your pride when you yourself are passing away?"

LIVE AND LET LIVE

Lee replied, "See how dogmatic you sound? Why can't you leave me alone? Live and let live, I say. I'm not condemning you nor condoning you. Yet, you've got me heading to hell. Where's the love in that?"

"Please listen to your humanism. It is exceedingly dogmatic. It purports to the idea of 'live and let live,' yet it often mocks God and defies faith, traditions, and spirituality. How is that not condemning Christians? You don't believe in a literal hell, but you consign Christians to an evolutionary dead end, a kind of hell on earth. Or you consign them to a kind of Purgatory of irrelevance and marginalization, where you make them suffer for their beliefs until they recant or at least live according to your views. Where's the love in that?

"But for me to point out your sin is love. For God to send His Son to die for those sins is love. For you to hear the gospel so patiently expressed to you, with its sober warnings, is also love."

"Can't we find some kind of common ground?" asked Lee. "Why does everything have to be one way or the other? Why not both?"

"Jesus said, 'I am the way, the truth, and the life. No one comes to the father except through me.' There is only one way to God, and it's God's way; it's God's Son. You see that as restrictive. I see it as an invitation to life! I see it as Jesus pointing you to the right path, the path that leads to life. That's not exclusivism, that's mercy and kindness in the midst of confusion and misdirection that leads many astray."

"But," asked Lee, "what about all those who have never heard of Jesus? What happened to them?"

"In your humanist worldview they died and became dirt for someone else's life to take root in. But the Bible teaches that God will judge justly according to each person's life, good and bad. Not all people are as bad as others. Yet, no one can earn salvation by being good. So, those who died without faith in the God of the Bible died without hope. They will face a just Judge according to their deeds."

"That doesn't seem fair," complained Lee. "God saves some and condemns others. Who wants a God like that?"

"All people deserve the same fate. All have sinned and fall short of what God requires. Left to themselves, all would be judged by their deeds and fall short of salvation. *That's God's justice.*

"But God determined to provide a way of salvation because He loves

His human creation. So, He withholds His hand of judgement to give people an opportunity to repent. *That's God's mercy.*

"Not all people have the same opportunity. Not all people who hear the gospel respond to it. Not all people come to faith in Christ. *That's God's sovereignty.* You would deny God His sovereignty, but God will be God!

"Then, with those who believe in Christ, God applies to them the work Jesus did on the cross to cover the guilt and penalty their sins deserved. They receive forgiveness, and are accepted into God's family, and receive an inheritance in glory and in the new heavens and new earth to come. *That's God's grace.*"

"But," said Lee, "what about what I want? Doesn't God care about my views? I have to agree to His view without any reference to mine. That seems oppressive to me."

"You simply don't see your rebellion, do you? God is God. He is not the one who needs to change. He hasn't done wrong. He has been patient and kind. You must change. You must turn from your own way. You must go home to God like the prodigal son went home to his father. God will embrace you, love you, forgive you, celebrate you, but you must return.

"Humanism, for all its claims to goodness and positivity, is a selfish philosophy that hardens people toward God and toward repentance. You must see that system of thought as shackling you to a prison in which you'll sit awaiting God's wrath. Cry out to God, now! He will open the door and set you free. Jesus said all who sin are slaves of sin, but if He sets you free, you will be truly free."

"Funny," said Lee, "I feel free now."

"Sin is deceptive and blinding. Sin gives a false view of reality and hardens the heart against God. Don't act upon your feelings. Act upon the word of God, upon the message of Jesus. Trust God's word over mans."

"I don't know that I can," said Lee.

"You need a radical change of heart. Jesus spoke of being born again. He was referring to a spiritual new birth. You need God's Spirit to help you believe. The change people need is not philosophical, technological, psychological, mechanical, governmental, or social, it's spiritual. It involves the mind, the will, and the emotions. It's a radical internal change of heart that results in knowing God and in a personal relationship with God through His loving Son.

"This birth is not an emotional or psychological state of mind, either.

It's a spiritual encounter with the living God that changes a person forever."

"I don't understand," replied Lee. "How is one born like that?"

"Believe in the Lord Jesus Christ and you will be saved. That's what the Bible says. And, it says this: if you confess with your lips that Jesus is Lord and believe in your heart that God raised Him from the dead, then you will be saved.

"For, after Jesus died on the cross for sins, three days later He rose from the dead. By that resurrection God showed that He validated Jesus as His Son and His death as an atonement, a covering for sin."

Lee said, "Well, I'll have to think about it. You're asking me to leave my friends and even my family."

"Yes, sometimes trusting Christ is costly. But it's not as costly as losing your soul."

DECISION TIME

Suddenly, some of Lee's friends from the Humanist Club showed up. They wondered who this person was talking to Lee. When they found out, confrontation ensued. A couple of angry students spoke up.

One man sternly declared, "So you're the one who has been filling Lee's mind with a lot of rubbish? Don't you have churches to preach your garbage in?"

Another person said, "Don't talk like that. They just want to impose their irrational and impossible views on us." Then, looking at the stranger, she said, "Your belief in an all-powerful deity is a myth and irrational. To hold such views means you are psychologically unstable. So, go away! Leave Lee alone!"

"I know you think you are wise beyond your years, but you are not. In reality, you are misguided and given over to the passions of your youth. And you are misleading others.

"So, let me put it to you as straightforwardly as I can. I know you are acting in ignorance, but God is calling you to repent! Turn from your own way to the God who loved you enough to send His Son to die for your sins. For God has fixed a day when He will judge the world in righteousness. And He has appointed His Son, Jesus Christ, as the Judge."

The crowd replied with vociferous grumbling. Their eyes were filled with anger toward the stranger, who felt as if violence might ensue.

"You sin against love, God's love, the greatest love! And you want to play God! You want to be God! You refuse to see it, but you want people to follow *you* and fawn over how clever you are in skirting God in your life. But you have rebelled against God.

"Does the force and urgency of my words surprise you? Listen, I have seen men on their deathbed with their knees knocking for fear of what will come next. Yet, they refused to repent, they refused to confess their sins to God, to admit to Him that they had done wrong. They cherished their pride more than God!

"These are serious and eternal matters! They rise above you and what you want, to God and what He rightly requires. Don't you understand? God is *commanding* you to surrender your will to His by following His Son as Lord and Savior."

Then, the stranger looked Lee straight in the eyes and said in front of them all, **"Lee, I have honestly and sincerely pointed you to your God. Through our discussions, God is calling you! Who will you serve? Will it**

be the empty promises of humanism with its course of rebellion against God? Or will it be the God of love, mercy, and grace, who made you, loves you, and gave His Son to redeem you?"

The crowd looked at Lee.

Lee looked at the crowd and then at the stranger.

A rare moment of eternal significance had descended. Everyone felt it. This decision constitutes the most radical change a person can make. Lee knew it. He knew how radical it would be to walk away from his humanism and embrace Christ.

What will Lee do?

What will *you* do?

POSTFACE

In the end, the present choices we make have eternal consequences. To live purely in the moment is neither wise nor good for yourself or others. God invites everyone to return to Him through the love and grace He has shown in His Son. To know God, love God, and be loved and known by God in a personal relationship with Him through His Son, is the true fulfillment of the meaning of life. Experiencing His grace and peace within results in a radical change so great that it reorients the mind and soul to that place of stability, satisfaction, and joy that human beings were created to know.

> *If you are not a Christian, please take a moment before reading on to ponder the Christian message expressed above.*

POSTLUDE – A MESSAGE TO SCIENTISTS

In concluding the main part of this book, I add to the story a direct message to scientists. Since science is held up as the authority for secular humanists, how does nature compare to the Christian worldview? Christians claim that God created science and all things. And so, does science affirm faith in God?

As scientists, we take great pride in logic and reason and in attempting to validate our work. Obviously, not all theories can be validated by direct observation. Yet, logic still applies to them, and one principle of logic is especially critical — the principle of non-contradiction.

Non-contradiction says that A cannot be A and not A at the same time in the same circumstances. That makes sense to us. Violating that law leads to absurdities. And we observe its truth in general science.

In the above story, I mentioned quantum mechanics. Let's consider some principles of science that I believe helps demonstrate the consistency of Christianity and the inconsistency of secular humanism.

First, consider that quantum mechanics demonstrate that there are valid energy states within which particles or quanta exist, and these states can be expressed mathematically. Such states demonstrate orderliness. So, in a very simplistic way, given a set of conditions, there are valid states for which nature is found to express itself.

Second, consider that the two fundamental principles of special relativity are that the laws of nature are always observed from an inertial reference frame and the speed of light is constant when measured within that reference frame. This, too, constitutes conditions that express valid states within which physical phenomena take place.

Both quantum mechanics and special relativity demonstrate the universe has consistency to it, and that consistency is observable. Similarly, other fields of science demonstrate that same consistency.

Now, let me introduce another set of principles. We'll call it the Law of Moral Hegemony (I'll explain why later). Let's propose that this law says that God's moral law is the only set of valid states within which a human being can act to be righteous and just before God. Furthermore, this law must always be observed for a human to be righteous and just before God. I maintain that this law exists and is just as observable in life as the laws of nature, only moral laws find expression through the beliefs and behaviors of people.

So here are three ideas that are all similar in that they involve valid states. Next, let's think about what it means to violate those states.

First, is it possible to violate states in nature? It may be possible to observe things that appear contradictory, but appearances are not reality. We presume that the laws of nature are never truly violated. And let's face it, if nature is not consistent, then, for the secular humanist, science is no certain authority for matters of life.

However, nature is consistent. For example, what we observe as chaos is actually the laws of nature worked out in extremely complex ways that we cannot make sense of from our observations. Yet at no time during the apparent chaos are the laws of nature being violated.

As another example, we may say that a person attempts to "defy the laws of gravity" by jumping off a cliff and flapping his arms like a bird. But really the law of gravity is never violated by the act — even if he managed to stay aloft!

In other words, as we observe reality in nature, we see that the laws of nature are consistent. They do not contradict each other. They demonstrate a set of valid states within which all the bits of nature act.

Now, is this idea true for the Law of Moral Hegemony I stated? Yes, but also, so it would seem, no. That's the key to understanding what makes human life special in relationship to God.

Yes, there is a set of valid states within which a person can act and be righteous and just before God. And, no, those states are not inviolable; a person can violate them, but only *apparently*.

Here's how it works. Let's summarize God's moral laws with the Ten Commandments. That would be a Christian's view of the boundaries enforced by the Law of Moral Hegemony. The idea of hegemony refers to God's authority as God to create as He chooses and to establish laws consistent with His own character and being. Such hegemony exists as well with God's design in the laws of nature, but when we think of morality we think more directly of authority or hegemony.

Within the boundaries of God's moral laws there are an infinite number of valid states. Very simplistically, one example would be that a man can marry any woman he wants to so long as she consents and they both satisfy the conditions of God's moral laws. These boundaries establish the freedom of one's will by establishing valid states, as it were, that one can choose from.

We might even say that valid choices within the boundaries of God's moral laws relate in concept to valid states in quantum mechanics or to the idea in special relativity that nature's laws are always obeyed.

Nature cannot break its own laws. Nature works consistently within those laws. However, people can break God's moral laws, and they do. The breaking of God's moral laws is called sin. This is where the Law of Moral Hegemony appears to differ from the laws of nature, but in truth doesn't.

At no time can the laws of nature be violated. We say that there are consequences in trying to violate them. For example, the man who jumps off a cliff and flaps his arms like a bird will probably suffer the consequence of death. Yet, gravity didn't commit any violation of itself. Gravity quietly did what God created it to do.

People, however, can appear to violate God's moral laws by choosing to act contradictory to them. If God says, "Yes," people can say, "No." And if God says, "No," people can say, "Yes." However, in doing so they fall short of being righteous and just before God, they sin, and they incur the genuine and real consequences of violating God's moral laws.

Sin allows a person to "flap his arms like a bird to defy gravity," so to speak. The sinner seems to go on happily without any apparent adverse effects. But the consequences will come. One cannot defy God's moral laws without consequences.

The man defying gravity sinks downward until he crashes. So too, the sinner defying God's moral laws sinks downward until he dies and stands before the Judge to receive sentence for his choices and actions.

The deception of sin is that it gives the illusion that God doesn't care or doesn't exist because the sentence against the sin is not executed immediately. But the truth is, as surely as the laws of nature cannot be violated, neither can God's moral laws.

What many scientists either reject or don't understand is that there is consistency between God's natural laws and God's moral laws. These are two sets of laws. They are different in how they operate, but both laws are observable. Natural laws operate on the physical. Moral laws operate on the soul and are expressed through the physical. Both laws are, therefore, observable.

Furthermore, both natural and moral laws are the product of God's mind. His authority (hegemony) established both. The existence of such laws and the necessity of their being obeyed are the result of God's will and authority. So, if it is vain to try and violate God's natural laws, so it is vain to try and violate His moral laws. Attempting to violate natural laws has immediate consequences that can be observed. Attempting to violate moral laws has just as real consequences, only the full impact of those consequences won't be felt or observed until Judgment Day.

So, the overall point I'm trying to make here is to show that all of God's laws — natural and moral — are consistent within any frame of reference. There is no equivocating or violating of non-contradiction. Murder cannot be murder and not murder. Lying cannot be lying and not lying. Sexual immorality cannot be and not be at the same time just because people choose to act in different cultural contexts or by self-established moral frameworks.

People simply cannot establish their own moral laws any more than we can invent new laws of nature. We may observe a new law of nature, but the law was already in existence. However, we do not discover new moral laws at all. Rather, moral laws must be revealed to us by God. Then we seek to understand them more and more.

Herein we observe further that there are things that we can know with certainty only because God reveals them. That implies it is more necessary to know the things that relate to the soul than to the body. Therefore, God's revelation of moral laws demonstrates the certainty of them to us and our necessity to know them. In other words, that God revealed the Ten Commandments and wrote them down with His own finger, highlights their absolute importance as a reference point in life.

Keep in mind that God is always true and fully trustworthy, and all that He reveals about Himself and us is for our good.

Therefore, the idea of moral relativism is truly absurd. It ignores God's revelation and makes morality emanate from within each person. That very idea violates the principle of non-contradiction, as something can at the same time be "moral" for one person and "immoral" for another. For example, it leaves open the possibility that Hitler was right and wrong at the same time. It lets morality change and shift such that right and wrong become merely the opinions of those in power. It leads to absurdity.

Furthermore, moral relativism is inconsistent with the laws of nature. Nature reveals absolutes, not relativism. Relativity is not relativism! Relativity demonstrates the same consistency as God's moral laws reveal. Relativism is merely the apparent violation of God's moral law. It's the flapping of arms to defy gravity when all along one is heading faster and faster to the rocky crags below!

Moral relativism leaves a person in a state of contradiction and inconsistency. Sadly, the human heart is often blind to those problems and a kind of moral fog overcomes the mind to leave a person justifying behavior that in other contexts they know is wrong.

Now, let us return to God's moral laws. If it is true that sinners are not righteous and just before God because they violate His moral laws, then how can sinners be made morally right with God? If all people have sinned, then how can they be sin and not sin at the same time? How can there be any hope for a sinner? The answer lies in God alone and not in the sinner.

There is no way for a sinner to be a sinner and not a sinner at the same time. That's absurd! But it's not absurd for God to give to a sinner a righteous and just standing on the basis of what He Himself (the Judge) did for the sinner. Enter Jesus Christ, God's Son.

Sin violates God's moral laws and must be punished. There are unavoidable consequences to sin. However, if those consequences are absorbed by another, then God can be both just in punishing sin and merciful in letting the sinner go free. That's exactly what God did by the cross of Jesus Christ. There on the cross, Jesus, who knew no sin, became sin for us, so that in Him we can become righteous and just before God.

The gospel of Jesus Christ is God's awesome revelation of wisdom and grace in how He does for sinners what they cannot do for themselves. And, because the gospel reveals something so glorious about the Person and love of God, it elevates moral laws to a special place above natural laws. Moral laws become more important to human beings than natural laws.

So, a sinner cannot be a sinner and not a sinner at the same time. However, a sinner can be a sinner and righteous and just before God at the same time when trusting Jesus as Savior! This is because Jesus takes our penalty and gives us His perfect righteousness as a gift. The sinner is justified by the blood and righteousness of the sinless Son of God. The sinner is made to stand justified before God by the righteousness of God Himself! The real and true consequences of sin are taken up by God Himself through Jesus His Son. In all this the grace of God is magnified!

This exchange — our sins for Christ's righteousness — takes place solely based on faith. Yes, faith, the very thing many impugn as subjective or not reasonable, is the basis upon which God justifies sinners. Faith sets humans apart from animals and from nature itself. Faith is relational, demonstrating confidence in God, reliance upon His mercy, and love for Him who first loved us. Faith, therefore, is not only reasonable, but also of greater importance to human life than pure reason alone. Reason may be the soil in which a seed is planted, but faith is the water and sunshine that makes it grow.

Faith, therefore, does not emanate viscerally from the flesh, but from the soul. Faith is not an animal instinct, but a means by which we commune with God. By faith we can know God as He is revealed by the Bible and in Jesus Christ. By faith we can live righteous and justified before God. By faith we seek to live out the laws of God as an act of love and devotion to the One who sets us free from sin. Far from being mere opinion or subjectivism, true faith sees life rightly because it sees God in all of life. Faith, therefore, makes sense of all things because God makes sense of all things.

So, my fellow scientists reading this, do you see the consistency and awesome, lovely beauty of God's wisdom and grace? I hope you do. I hope you see His amazing love for sinners. I hope you see the primacy of faith in God as He has revealed Himself. And I hope you will choose to trust Jesus as your Savior.

The Christian faith is consistent. And on the Day of Judgment there will be no excuses, only the frightening reality that God's moral laws are fixed and cannot be violated. The only way you and I can survive the consequences of our sins is by accepting by faith what God Himself did to redeem and restore us.

Accept and receive Jesus today as your Savior and then follow Him as your Lord. And consider what the Lord promises, "You will seek me and find me when you search for me with all your heart" (Jeremiah 29:13).

APPENDIX – NOTES AND COMMENTS

In this appendix, I discuss some of the reasoning behind the above story and message. I also seek to explain things a little more fully from a Christian perspective in areas I felt would be too much to put into the story. I give some supporting thoughts from the Bible for the Christian positions expressed in the story. God's word is my ultimate authority and so I firmly take my stand upon it. Psalm 119:130 says, "The revelation of your words brings light and gives understanding to the inexperienced."

INTRODUCTION

The reason secular humanism is a powerful persuasion today is that it appeals to the natural man; that is, it appeals to our fallen human nature.[1] Hence, one of the purposes of this book is to argue for a new nature, one regenerated by the Spirit of God, renewed in the knowledge of God, and transformed or changed.[2] That constitutes the truly radical change that is signified in the Bible by conversion. Just look at the Apostle Paul for example. There is a man who, in a transforming moment, went from persecuting and trying to destroy the Church to being its greatest champion.[3]

RADICAL CHANGE

I introduce the debate with some thoughts intended to orient the reader to the issues at hand. What is secular humanism? I introduce it, and then the rest of the book constitutes my logical outworking of it as it relates to many of the issues of life.

The idea of "radical change" is introduced as well. It's a phrase that both sides can claim. From a secular point of view, it is certainly "radical" to walk away from religion. But it is more radical when sinners come to Christ, because the transformation of the human heart by the Holy Spirit is far more

---

[1] "But the person without the Spirit [natural man] does not receive what comes from God's Spirit, because it is foolishness to him; he is not able to understand it since it is evaluated spiritually" (1 Corinthians 2:14).

[2] "Therefore, if anyone is in Christ, he is a new creation; the old has passed away, and see, the new has come!" (2 Corinthians 5:17).

[3] Acts 9:1-9; 26:12-18. Also, 1 Timothy 1:13-ff, "Even though I was formerly a blasphemer, a persecutor, and an arrogant man. But I received mercy because I acted out of ignorance in unbelief … This saying is trustworthy and deserving of full acceptance: 'Christ Jesus came into the world to save sinners' — and I am the worst of them."

radical than changing one's worldview.[4]

A SECULAR UNIVERSE

I have heard scientists propose that the universe may collapse in upon itself and then form again through another Big Bang. Thus, we have the idea of an oscillating universe. Obviously, this would take place over many billions of years. Such a view does seem like a logical conclusion of believing that matter has always existed.

It is interesting that the secular view of the universe ascribes to it attributes that belong to God alone. Particularly the attributes of self-existence, eternality, and independence. The Bible ascribes those attributes to God.[5] One major difference between the secular view and the biblical view is that the material universe has no personality, it doesn't speak. Nor does the material universe have a will or emotion or consciousness (contrary to what some science fiction ideas might imply). God, on the other hand, is an awesome Person and reveals Himself to us in several ways. He also has a will, emotion, feeling, and attributes such as love, goodness, wrath, and so on. There is simply no comparison between knowing the impersonal universe and knowing the personal God who created it! He is the self-existent Being who called all things into being and sustains them.[6]

The age of the earth is indeed a debate among Christians. But this Christian sees no reason to abandon a young earth. Imagine how the laws of nature must have behaved as God unfolded the universe at creation when He spoke it into being. We can imagine that the speed of light, for example, was not what we measure today, but like the speed of sound in air, it varied with conditions, those conditions relating to the fabric of spacetime as it expanded

---

[4] "Everyone who remains in him does not sin; everyone who sins has not seen him or known him" (1 John 3:6). John is here referring to the fact that sin is not dominating the Christian as a way of life, as a practice. He is not saying Christians never sin (c.f. 1 John 1:8-10). But notice here the radical transformation of the sinner!

[5] Exodus 3:14; Psalm 90:1-2; Isaiah 43:11.

[6] "By faith we understand that the universe was created by the word of God, so that what is seen was made from things that are not visible" (Hebrews 11:3). "For everything was created by him, in heaven and on earth, the visible and the invisible, whether thrones or dominions or rulers or authorities — all things have been created through him and for him. He is before all things, and by him all things hold together" (Colossians 1:16-17).

outward by God's command to fill its present place. Furthermore, imagine that if it is possible to travel beyond the speed of light — perhaps entering some type of altered spacetime — that gets one to a faraway galaxy, then that galaxy would actually be not much different than we observe it right now. That thought makes space travel more exciting to this author.

But I understand that it is hard to imagine of time any differently than how we perceive it today. Thus, it is understandable how tempting it is to think of the processes of the beginnings of the universe as happening at a pace that we experience today. Hence, we perceive many billions and billions of years must have taken place. Hence, we interpret astronomical and geological data by the measurements of time we experience today. That's understandable.

Now, imagine thinking quite differently about time.[7] Imagine the beginning of the universe by God's voice that spoke it dramatically and instantly into existence. We do not experience such power today; although it was demonstrated by Jesus Christ.[8] Think of God's speaking matter into existence as like a bomb exploding — only with the effect of formation rather than destruction. For a very brief moment there are rapid transient phenomena happening, and then soon it reaches a calm, steady-state condition. Call it the "Big Bang" if you want to, but it was God's command speaking all things into existence out of nothing and directing those things into their current state. The debate on age boils down to how long those transients lasted. I see no reason to doubt they were truly rapid, as the biblical account indicates by the word "day" in Genesis 1.

Those initial rapid transient changes are long gone; perhaps seen, however, in very distant astronomical observations. Now things are steady-state. Time moves on at a different pace, so to speak, than when creation obeyed the voice of its Creator and came into being. Now the Creator is present exercising His will and power in maintaining and governing all He made — we call that God's divine Providence through His divine Presence.

Consider this as well. In the story I make the point that science cannot go back in time to observe origins. So, it makes sense that we would rely upon God telling us what happened. My view is that the Bible reveals the message

---

[7] "Dear friends, don't overlook this one fact: With the Lord one day is like a thousand years, and a thousand years like one day" (2 Peter 3:8).

[8] Turning water into wine; calming the sea instantly; miraculous healings; raising the dead.

of a young earth. I grant that that does not necessarily prove the universe or earth are young, because as I said, even Christians disagree on this. But to ignore the Bible is to ignore God revealing to us His awesome will and power in creation; it is to ignore the fundamental truth about our origins that must orient our thinking and guide our scientific interpretations.[9]

Maybe God doesn't reveal to us all the details of creation and hence He doesn't require that we know them. But, He does require that our faith rest on His word to guide us in our thinking. It is my contention that if more scientists would faithfully embrace the biblical records, then greater progress would be made in understanding ourselves and our world than can ever be made with a secular assumption.

THE NATURE OF MANKIND

The science of DNA is discovering new things all the time. I know only bits about it. However, one thing is certain; the DNA structure stores an amazing amount of information. It is certainly not unreasonable to see design in that. There is so much purpose in the DNA, so much diversity of a kind of species, so much ability to adapt for the good of the organism, that to this author it screams God's wisdom! I am left bowing in humble worship when I learn new things about DNA and its capabilities.[10]

One more comment about genetics that I have experienced while writing genetic algorithms (GAs) to solve optimization problems. When I first encountered GAs, I was fascinated that such algorithms could be written. But after writing my own and working with the concepts, something became very apparent. Even if chromosome crossover and mutation are random, even if we devise various schemes for selection, I write the objective function. I determine the value of something that is to be selected. In a sense, my design drives the algorithm. So, where in nature is such an objective function? It seems to me that the laws of thermodynamics would tend toward simplicity and lower energy as an objective — not what would tend toward the level of complexity we see in life! Thus, in my mind, genetic processes argue for design and for the divine wisdom of God. We may imitate

---

[9] "They deliberately overlook this: By the word of God the heavens came into being long ago and the earth was brought about from water and through water" (2 Peter 3:5).

[10] "I will praise you because I have been remarkably and wondrously made" (Psalm 139:14).

them, but they are not the product of random chance.[11]

Regarding the nature of animals and humans, we observe a distinction between the instinct for survival and the ability to reason ethically through situations. Animals are driven by a visceral instinct to survive. This instinct is observable in pets, as in the wild. Yet, people are able to come to more complex decisions that give evidence to a distinguishing nature that points us back to God. I am referring to the idea of ethical decisions; decisions that relate to right and wrong, to how we affect the lives of others, and so on. Human nature has the ability to reflect upon the Law of God because we are made in the image of God. That added dimension makes us distinct from the animal kingdom and points beyond genetics to God's design.[12] It also gives evidence to the Bible's revelation that God put mankind in charge of the animals and this world, as their stewards.[13]

Over the years I have heard intellectuals describe religion as irrational. However, it is quite rational to believe God as He has revealed Himself. In fact, it's irrational not to! Some secular humanists have questioned the sanity of Christians, as the student did in the story, and as some have been known to do in history. But where's the sanity in going against God?[14]

BODY AND SOUL

The study of complexity is fascinating. I can imagine it is alluring to the secular mind as an answer to some of the difficult questions of life. But, consider that behind complexity there is a great deal of smarts, of logic, of purpose, all of which point to a Designer. Consider as well that complexity is simplicity to God. His wisdom and understanding take our breath away, yet He still loves and cares about us.[15]

---

[11] See Job 38.
[12] "Consider the birds of the sky: They don't sow or reap or gather into barns, yet your heavenly Father feeds them. Aren't you worth more than they?" (Matthew 6:26).
[13] "God blessed them, and God said to them, 'Be fruitful, multiply, fill the earth, and subdue it. Rule the fish of the sea, the birds of the sky, and every creature that crawls on the earth'" (Genesis 1:28).
[14] "The fool says in his heart, 'There's no God'" (Psalm 14:1).
[15] ""For my thoughts are not your thoughts, and your ways are not my ways." This is the Lord's declaration" (Isaiah 55:8).

And consider that the soul is the gift of God to human beings.[16] The soul is how people can know God in a personal way. The soul does not die. Through the soul, God has set eternity in our hearts so that we know that there's more to reality than this life now.[17] It is through the soul that we have a consciousness of God such that even if we deny Him it is only by suppressing that knowledge of God that we do it.[18]

CULTURE

I can imagine that there are humanistic arguments that explain with more clarity that Hitler was wrong. But I am attempting to use the logic of survival of the fittest to show that from a purely secular view ethics ultimately boils down to a battle of wills. Ethics become the opinions of people. There is no outside authority, and science itself cannot cover matters beyond its purview.

As an example of the limitation of science, consider that science clearly reveals male and female genders, and yet people ignore that and argue for transgenderness. Furthermore, scientific observation makes it quite clear that a male and female body belong together in a sexual relationship, yet people ignore that and have homosexual encounters. This simply demonstrates to this author that people don't really stand on science for ethics, but on opinions and feelings and on what they want. To me, this as an example of how people, including scientists, will sometimes interpret data to fit their own worldview.

But remember this, all people sin, and no sin is ultimately more damning than another.[19] Furthermore, all people struggle with different sins. One person is attracted to the same sex, another to the opposite sex, but both in an inordinate way — in violation of God's law on marriage between one man and

---

[16] "Then the Lord God formed the man out of the dust from the ground and breathed the breath of life into his nostrils, and the man became a living being" (Genesis 2:7). The clear implication of this verse is that Adam was created not only differently than the animals, but with a soul from God's breath to become a living being.

[17] Ecclesiastes 3:11.

[18] Romans 1:18-20.

[19] "For whoever keeps the entire law, and yet stumbles at one point, is guilty of breaking it all" (James 2:10).

one woman.[20] Some people are driven by greed or power. Some are tempted to excess with food or even legitimate activities that ultimately replace God in their life. All this is sin. It's wrong to single out one sin against another.[21] God takes all sin very seriously because it violates His character and the way He created us.[22]

Why do we sin? Yes, it's because of our fallen human nature. But it's also because we are not satisfied with God. Let me explain. Sin can be like a drug. We take the drug to make us feel better about ourselves, about our life, our circumstances. Our desire for deep satisfaction, pleasure, peace, relief from pain, can be a motivation to sin. The truth is that culture can make sin even easier by removing those moral standards of behavior that restrict sin and point us to God. That's why as a society turns its back on God, sin becomes more prevalent. Righteousness begins to look odd. People become happy and content to go their own way, since there appears to be nothing to hinder them.

But God would have us find our ultimate satisfaction in Him. To know Him and His love doesn't remove sin, but it does displace temptation by giving us a better course of life to follow. Knowing that God loved me and died for me to bring me to Himself means more to me than sin.[23] It doesn't mean I never sin, but it means sin doesn't dominate me anymore.[24] Now, God's love for me motivates me and I'm growing to love Him more each day.[25] That's

---

[20] "This is why a man leaves his father and mother and bonds with his wife, and they become one flesh" (Genesis 2:24). Sexual union is truly a beautiful and wonderful gift from God. But it only pleases God when done in the bonds of the marriage covenant between one man and one woman! See also Hebrews 13:4.

[21] Notice in the following passage that Paul doesn't single out any particular sin. And notice how he uses the past tense to emphasize what Christians were but have now become by faith in Christ. "Don't you know that the unrighteous will not inherit God's kingdom? Do not be deceived: No sexually immoral people, idolaters, adulterers, or males who have sex with males, no thieves, greedy people, drunkards, verbally abusive people, or swindlers will inherit God's kingdom. And some of you used to be like this. But you were washed, you were sanctified, you were justified in the name of the Lord Jesus Christ and by the Spirit of our God" (1 Corinthians 6:9-11).

[22] "Everyone who commits sin practices lawlessness; and sin is lawlessness" (1 John 3:4).

[23] "I have been crucified with Christ, and I no longer live, but Christ lives in me. The life I now live in the body, I live by faith in the Son of God, who loved me and gave himself for me" (Galatians 2:20).

[24] Romans 6:14.

[25] 2 Corinthians 5:14.

where God wants us to be as human beings made in His image. He wants us to experience His love so that it grips our heart with love and devotion to Him as our response.[26]

FAITH AND SCIENCE

It may be that some secular scientists will acknowledge the role of faith as I describe here. So be it. Faith then enters into their secular worldview as just another aspect of life. But the primacy of the role of faith speaks more directly to the Christian argument of reality than the secular one. For faith is central to Christianity.[27]

Furthermore, faith is confidence in something and the conviction that something is true even if all the details are not known. That's how the Bible defines faith in Hebrews 11:1, and it's a great definition. It easily translates to people who put the trust in science rather than God. They are exercising faith the same way that Christians are. They have confidence in something they don't fully see or understand. Yet, for the Christian, God speaks to us. For the secular humanist, nature only speaks through them, so their own voice becomes a kind of self-fulfilling prophecy when it comes to metaphysical things. In a sense, therefore, secular humanists really have faith in themselves.[28] For, science cannot reach into areas of the past, the future beyond the grave, or into defining human meaning, without the conclusions ultimately becoming merely the opinions of person who holds them.

God's wisdom, however, speaks thusly, "Anyone who listens to me is happy, watching at my doors every day, waiting by the posts of my doorway. For the one who finds me finds life and obtains favor from the Lord, but the one who misses me harms himself; all who hate me love death" (Proverbs 8:34-36). This truth makes sense when we consider that God spoke to us directly through the Bible, taking all the guesswork out of the central issues of life: origins, destiny, and meaning.

---

[26] "Listen, Israel: The Lord our God, the Lord is one. Love the Lord your God with all your heart, with all your soul, and with all your strength" (Deuteronomy 6:4-5).
[27] "But the righteous one will live by his faith" (Habakkuk 2:4).
[28] "This is what the Lord says: Cursed is the person who trusts in mankind. He makes human flesh his strength, and his heart turns from the Lord" (Jeremiah 17:5).

AUTHORITY

The Apostle Paul writes, "For since, in God's wisdom, the world did not know God through wisdom ..." (1 Corinthians 1:21a). The implication of this statement is clear. The knowledge required for salvation cannot be discovered through the wisdom of philosophy, or what we call the scientific method, it must be *revealed* to us by God. That is exactly what God did through the Bible.[29]

This chapter is one of the most important in the book. I tried to express the secular point of view regarding how they believe we can know something. Yet again, it is completely rational and reasonable to study the Bible to know God. If the Bible is God's revelation, as Christians believe and as it says it is,[30] then it is a solid authority for knowing things within its purview, as in knowing God and the salvation He has provided.

The key point in this chapter is that the secular worldview leaves ultimate authority to the opinions of people, whereas the Bible is considered as God's word to all mankind. And so, in the Christian worldview, ultimate authority rests with God and we submit to Him by seeking Him through the Bible.

Now, it's true that the Bible is still read by people, and people can and do misinterpret it. But that problem lies not in the Bible but in us! It's important to take that into account. Christians are fallible and errant; the Bible is not.[31] That is a vitally important caveat when considering the Christian argument for the Bible as an authority on matters not in the direct purview of scientific discovery, matters relating to eternal life.

Furthermore, when we say we take the Bible as our authority we are not

---

[29] 2 Timothy 3:15, "And you know that from infancy you have known the sacred Scriptures, which are able to give you wisdom for salvation through faith in Christ Jesus."

[30] For example: Matthew 5:18; John 10:35; 2 Timothy 3:16; 2 Peter 1:20-21. Also 1 Corinthians 2:10, "Now God has revealed these things to us by the Spirit, since the Spirit searches everything, even the depths of God." It is also by God's Spirit that men wrote down that revelation (2 Peter 2:21).

[31] "The entirety of your word is truth, each of your righteous judgments endures forever" (Psalm 119:160). See also, "Lord, your testimonies are completely reliable" (Psalm 93:5). And note this warning by Peter about reading Paul's letters as it relates to all of Scripture: "He speaks about these things in all his letters. There are some things hard to understand in them. The untaught and unstable will twist them to their own destruction, as they also do with the rest of the Scriptures" (2 Peter 3:16).

worshiping a book — as some have accused us — but we are worshiping the God whose Spirit authored that book. We are therefore rightly placing ourselves under God's authority, seeking His will, and submitting ourselves humbly to His instruction. That is exactly the place God created human beings to be in![32]

RELEVANCE

One of the biggest misconceptions about Christianity is that somehow God is restricting people's lives by His laws. God's laws are for our good.[33] They reveal the boundaries of what He approves. They reveal how He made us to reflect His image and character. Thus, they also reveal our sins when we go beyond those boundaries. That's good. For it points us to our need for forgiveness, which God has abundantly provided for us through His Son.[34]

HERE AND NOW

Over the years I have heard many people speak toward the "here and now," not philosophically, but colloquially. Another example of a similar colloquialism is the phrase, "live for the moment." We see this in advertising that focuses on the moment, now, today. This idea permeates our culture, whereby people ignore eternity or put it off.

I made up this speech about the here and now by simply putting myself in the shoes of someone trying to get students excited about life from a secular humanist perspective. The here and now is implicitly the focus of humanism, so I simply expressed what I would say if I espoused that view.

---

[32] "He humbled you by letting you go hungry; then he gave you manna to eat, which you and your ancestors had not known, so that you might learn that man does not live on bread alone but on every word that comes from the mouth of the Lord" (Deuteronomy 8:3). Observe Christ's humble servant's heart as evidence of what God wants for all human beings, "Adopt the same attitude as that of Christ Jesus, who, existing in the form of God, did not consider equality with God as something to be exploited. Instead he emptied himself by assuming the form of a servant, taking on the likeness of humanity. And when he had come as a man, he humbled himself by becoming obedient to the point of death — even to death on a cross" (Philippians 2:5-8).
[33] Psalms 19 and 119 show how the law of the Lord is good.
[34] "For what the law could not do since it was weakened by the flesh, God did. He condemned sin in the flesh by sending his own Son in the likeness of sinful flesh as a sin offering" (Romans 8:3).

A BETTER WAY

I am convinced that mankind is getting worse, not better. I say this because of the testimony of Scripture.[35] The farther people drift from God, the worse things will become. This is because the real problem lies not in culture or the Bible, but in the human heart. The whole battle between Christianity and secular humanism shows the downward spiral I'm speaking of. People in the modern world have turned their backs on God, perhaps more than any time since the Noahic Flood, even though information about God is more accessible today than at any other time in history.

If people would only stop and consider the emptiness of focusing on the "here and now," I'm sure they would start seeking God more directly and personally. He is not far from anyone, as the Bible says.[36]

INSTITUTIONAL ADVANCEMENT

Many people forget that Christianity started many of the great institutions of learning and has pioneered helping people who are poor or down-and-out. The Church has this mission because learning reflects how God made us. Understanding His world brings Him glory (or at least it should), as we give Him the praise and honor He deserves. And Christianity has always championed helping the poor as a cornerstone of its ministry.[37]

Karl Marx is the one who called religion an opiate of the masses.[38] Yet, when you think about it, that's not at all what Christianity is teaching or promoting, that's what socialism promises. Socialism is all about giving to the masses what will quiet them down and make them feel good and make them support their leaders. Christianity is all about salvation, love to God, and loving others as yourself. It impacts society and culture by living out those principles.

Love is the goal of Christianity.[39] Socialism is self-centered and leaves

---

[35] See Romans 1:18-ff; Romans 3:10-18. And consider Ecclesiastes 7:29, "Only see this: I have discovered that God made people upright, but they pursued many schemes."

[36] "He did this so that they might seek God, and perhaps they might reach out and find him, though he is not far from each one of us" (Acts 17:27).

[37] "Happy is one who is considerate of the poor; the Lord will save him in a day of adversity" (Psalm 41:1).

[38] https://en.wikipedia.org/wiki/Opium_of_the_people.

[39] "Now the goal of our instruction is love that comes from a pure heart, a good conscience, and a sincere faith" (1 Timothy 1:5).

people focusing on themselves and what they can get from the government. Christianity can thrive in any governmental environment because its focus is upon God and others.[40]

In socialism, government becomes a kind of "god" to the people. In Christianity, God is God, and knowing Him and His love is itself the greatest and most wonderful thing in the world. And when people truly come to know God and have tasted His love, there's nothing this world can offer or do to make them leave the God they love. Class distinctions, racial differences, economic disparities, begin to fade away when true Christian love emanates from within a person because Christ's grace makes believers focus on the mercy they have received, on their unity in Christ, and on the fact that He shows no favoritism.[41]

Concerning those who profess Christ and fall away, I add this thought about the necessity of repentance. The Apostle Paul states that salvation is by faith alone[42] but always results in a process the Bible calls sanctification.[43] That process is the evidence of repentance. It is "putting off" sin and "putting on" a holy life, righteousness, conformity to God's Law.[44] That doesn't mean perfection in this life, but it does mean a continual growth in Christ's likeness reflected in the believer's life. That's why Christians are "human becomings." We are in the process of becoming more and more like our Savior. That process won't be completed until we get to heaven.[45]

---

[40] "Let everyone submit to the governing authorities, since there is no authority except from God, and the authorities that exist are instituted by God" (Romans 13:1). And consider 1 Peter 2:17, "Honor everyone. Love the brothers and sisters. Fear God. Honor the emperor."

[41] "There is no Jew or Greek, slave or free, male and female; since you are all one in Christ Jesus" (Galatians 3:28). "Making every effort to keep the unity of the Spirit through the bond of peace" (Ephesians 4:3). And, "For there is no favoritism with God" (Romans 2:11).

[42] "For we conclude that a person is justified by faith apart from the works of the law" (Romans 3:28).

[43] "But we ought to thank God always for you, brothers and sisters loved by the Lord, because from the beginning God has chosen you for salvation through sanctification by the Spirit and through belief in the truth" (2 Thessalonians 2:13).

[44] Ephesians 4:20-24.

[45] "Not that I have already reached the goal or am already perfect, but I make every effort to take hold of it because I also have been taken hold of by Christ Jesus" (Philippians 3:12).

BLAME GAME

One of the patterns I've observed over the years is that sometimes secular humanists give the impression that it's only the "other side" that is doing anything wrong. There appears to be little self-reflection or consideration that "we're doing the same thing." Problems emanate from the human heart. Whatever people believe, when you study human nature, you'll find the same problems in Christian and non-Christian circles. That fact points us to the *common problem* of sin.

The whole debate about theocracy is overblown. It's true that there are some small groups of Christians who have theological positions that espouse a theocracy. But the Bible does not teach it. Even ancient Israel, which was to be a theocracy, is never put forth as a system to be imposed on other nations!

Romans 13 makes it clear that Christians are to be good citizens no matter what the government is like. For at the time Paul wrote that chapter he lived in the pagan Roman Empire. Nowhere does the Bible teach that Christians are to overthrow a government and start a theocracy.

The accusation of a theocracy by secular humanists (which I have personally encountered) is entirely a misunderstanding of how Christianity works. However, it seems to me that secular humanists often promote an a-theocracy, a secular government, and develop a fearmongering toward religion to justify their own view. Christians believe in influencing governments by their beliefs, but that allows for all beliefs to have influence. It strikes me that secular humanism wants to have only "secular" beliefs in government, thus isolating opposition and imposing their own agenda.

If some Christians have looked to government as a means to push the Christian faith on others, those individuals are rare. No Christian can believe that faith in Christ and love for God can be forced upon people by government. Christians don't view government that way, rather we seek to be "salt and light" in the world, as Jesus told us to be.[46] Some believers can do that through government. Being "salt and light" is a calling for each Christian in whatever vocation they are in, and it reflects the proper way Christian ideas are to influence others.

---

[46] Matthew 5:13.

PARTICULARS

All people have a creed, something they believe.[47] It is futile to think that Christians have a creed, but secular humanists don't. Everyone has a belief system, whether or not they can fully articulate it.

DIFFERENT STANDARDS

This chapter reflects upon the idea that God sees us in a manner that most people don't think about.[48] We tend to think we're a good person. We tend to judge ourselves by ourselves or others; we tend to compare ourselves to what others are doing. But that's not God's standard.[49]

It is imperative that people understand that God judges at a much deeper level. Even Christians don't fully understand their own heart. That's why the Bible teaches that the human heart is deceitful. Who can truly know it? Only God can.[50]

We need to understand that God has every right to judge people whom He created. I'm sure that trying to avoid dealing with God's judgment is one reason people argue for a secular world. They don't want to deal with issues of guilt. They don't want to face repentance or change. So, they adhere to ideas that make them feel comfortable in their behavior. But, needless to say, this is an eternally dangerous way of life.[51]

---

[47] The word creed is from the Latin, credo, meaning "I believe."
[48] "But the Lord said to Samuel, 'Do not look at his appearance or his stature because I have rejected him. Humans do not see what the Lord sees, for humans see what is visible, but the Lord sees the heart'" (1 Samuel 16:7).
[49] "An oracle within my heart concerning the transgression of the wicked person: Dread of God has no effect on him. For with his flattering opinion of himself, he does not discover and hate his iniquity. The words from his mouth are malicious and deceptive; he has stopped acting wisely and doing good. Even on his bed he makes malicious plans. He sets himself on a path that is not good, and he does not reject evil" (Psalm 36:1-4).
[50] Jeremiah 17:9.
[51] "For the wicked one boasts about his own cravings; the one who is greedy curses and despises the Lord. In all his scheming, the wicked person arrogantly thinks, 'There's no accountability, since there's no God'" (Psalm 10:3-4). "He says to himself, 'God has forgotten; he hides his face and will never see'" (verse 11). "Why has the wicked person despised God? He says to himself, 'You will not demand an account'" (verse 13).

RADICAL HUMANISM

This chapter introduces the harsher side of secular humanism. That's not to say that Christianity hasn't had its harsher moments in history — for example, the Crusades.[52] However, genuine Christianity brings true peace both to the heart and to a culture. People, not Christianity, bring pride, violence, prejudice, arrogance, and conceit to bear upon others. People must ultimately point the finger of accusation at themselves, not the God of the Bible. Mankind's problems do not fundamentally stem from social, racial, or economic issues, but from sin in the human heart![53]

So, when a worldview rejects God, then there's no telling where it will end up, despite its supposed best intentions. For, without a concept that one day a person will stand before God and give an account of one's self, then anything can be justified.[54] And, believing one will stand before God on their own terms does no good either. We must understand that God's law — summarized by the Ten Commandments — will be the standard against which God will measure the heart of everyone who ever lived.[55]

TRUTH AND CULTURE

Postmodernism highlights to this author the utter confusion that comes from a purely secular worldview. I've heard statements like "words have no meaning" or "truth is relative." One wonders where the confusion will end. Yet, for people who espouse the certainty of science as their authority, the trends of postmodern thinking seem contradictory. This all seems more to me like groping in the dark to find the light switch, when all along God is holding the candle that no one wants to look at.

Regarding the growth of Christian theology over time, one must consider

---

[52] I also mention abuses during the era of the Holy Romans Empire, when Church and State were one. Notably relevant to this book is the way the church treated the sun-centered views of Galileo Galilei. There were also spiritual abuses that led to the Protestant Reformation.

[53] "For from within, out of people's hearts, come evil thoughts, sexual immoralities, thefts, murders, adulteries, greed, evil actions, deceit, self-indulgence, envy, slander, pride, and foolishness" (Mark 7:21-22).

[54] And consider how oaths in a law court are made less significant when taken without reference to one day appearing before God to give an account.

[55] "Now we know that whatever the law says, it speaks to those who are subject to the law, so that every mouth may be shut and the whole world may become subject to God's judgment" (Romans 3:19).

that error has historically been the crucible within which Christian doctrine was refined. Western civilization didn't create Christian doctrine. That's a naive understanding. When the gospel was threatened by error, theologians honed their understanding of the Bible. This is nothing less that God's grace at work when Truth was threatened by error.[56]

CHURCH

The sermon preached here is from a sermon I wrote and preached in a church I once pastored. For people who don't understand God, I cannot think of a better way to show them God's heart than the parable of the Prodigal Son. This is one of the richest treasure stores of God's love found anywhere in the Bible. What an invitation from God to return to Him!

A FATHER'S LOVE

I made it a point to bring out that Lee's father abandoned him and his mother, because I believe such traumas are one reason people reject God. But do not impose the errors and sins of people onto God. Rather, take God as He is revealed in the Bible.

I grant that to a beginner not everything is clear in the Bible about God. It takes time to understand some of the historical and redemptive aspects of the Bible. Therefore, if you are new to the Bible, I would recommend starting with the New Testament and the Gospels — Matthew, Mark, Luke, and John. God's love and glory are revealed most clearly through His Son, Jesus. Don't be hung up on the unique historical judgments of God in the Old Testament, but rather, see them as illustrative of His willingness to have wrath upon sin. It takes some matured thinking and study to grasp the fullness of God's ways. Be patient with your own growth in understanding events in the Bible that don't make sense.

There are good answers to the difficult questions that some impose upon the Bible. Some people will focus upon those difficulties as evidence of errors in the Bible. This is understandable but unreasonable when good answers to those difficulties are ignored. When those answers are ignored by people who

---

[56] "When the Spirit of truth comes, he will guide you into all the truth. For he will not speak on his own, but he will speak whatever he hears. He will also declare to you what is to come" (John 16:13). This passage was spoken by Jesus to the Apostles giving evidence of the Spirit's inspiration of the Bible, but also indicating that through the Bible that same Spirit will guide the Church!

criticize the Bible, they are likely imposing a secular worldview upon the Bible. Once that is done, there is no way they will ever justify the supernatural or take the Bible seriously. They have already embarked upon a wandering in the desert of disagreement and will find little or nothing of value, for without faith it is impossible to please God (Hebrews 11:6).[57]

God is always didactic. But in the Old Testament, He was clearly more tactile in His dealings, much like a parent is to a young child. In the New Testament, He is even more didactic, much like an adult speaking to adults. Yet at all times, when He speaks, He expects us to listen to Him.

The divinity of Christ is a vital Christian doctrine. Only a divine Savior could possibly have borne upon Himself the full weight of God's wrath. Only a divine Savior could possibly have a righteousness that could make a sinner stand justified before a holy God by meeting God's own divine standards. Only a divine Savior could bring all who come to Him all the way to God, for He is God.

Christ is fully man and fully God. Therefore, He can perfectly represent us to God as our Savior, and he can perfectly represent God to us as our Lord. Come to Jesus and you come all the way to God — God the Son, the Second Person of the Triune Godhead (Father, Son, and Holy Spirit). The Trinity is a mystery only because we can't fully wrap our minds around such a God; but then, that's why He's God!

RESCUE MISSION - DAY ONE AND DAY TWO

Both speeches here are my attempts at expressing the secular humanist's worldview. As before, I try to put myself in the place of one believing this worldview and attempt to express it winsomely and rationally. I don't know how well I succeeded, but I made a sincere attempt.

Also, regarding the accusation that Christian experience is "psychological," I have encountered this myself. Many years ago, I had a long discussion about religion with an atheist. At the end I related to him my conversion experience and his response was, "That's just psychological." That is all that atheists can say. They must deny the reality of God's supernatural work in

---

[57] I would also encourage the reader to look up books that demonstrate the accuracy of the Bible by archeological evidence. There is an enormous amount of data that confirms or gives reasonable credibility to historical events and people mentioned in the Bible.

another human being. But that is certainly not a scientific approach. Genuine conversion is observable evidence of the supernatural. That is a fact. Even if such experiences can be faked or falsely claimed, that does not negate the reality of their presence in life and in agreement with what the Bible claims happens during conversion.

REBUTTAL

This chapter is a limited response to the challenges raised by the humanist conference speakers of the previous two chapters. My point here is not to answer everything, but to demonstrate how the Christian worldview adds information to basic human concerns because of how God made us and the revelation He has given to us in the Bible. To ignore God is to bring a person into eternal peril. I believe that and have made it my desire to warn readers of their danger and appeal to them to turn back to God.

LIVE AND LET LIVE

In this chapter, Lee is clearly getting tired of this debate, and yet to some degree he has nothing else to say. He is a nice person, and he is trying to end the arguments peacefully. That is commendable. However, Jesus' words are direct. The Bible is direct. All people everywhere must repent.[58] That is, we must turn from our own way back to God through Jesus, His Son. That truth cannot be accommodated to or compromised on. But we should see it as a *powerful invitation* by a loving and forgiving Savior.[59]

It is interesting how our culture is led by feelings and not faith. Eve let her feelings take precedence over her faith in God's word and it led to disaster. God would have us trust Him first. Faith must come first. Feelings always follow faith and obedience to God.[60]

Regarding the sovereignty of God mentioned in this chapter, the Bible

---

[58] "Therefore, having overlooked the times of ignorance, God now commands all people everywhere to repent" (Acts 17:30). "If anyone does not repent, he will sharpen his sword; he has strung his bow and made it ready" (Psalm 7:12).
[59] "Come to me, all of you who are weary and burdened, and I will give you rest. Take up my yoke and learn from me, because I am lowly and humble in heart, and you will find rest for your souls. For my yoke is easy and my burden is light" (Matthew 11:28-30).
[60] "For we walk by faith, not by sight" (2 Corinthians 5:7).

describes our Creator as the Potter and us as the clay.[61] Who can deny their Maker His rights over what He makes? God's sovereignty should deeply humble us. He is very gracious, but He is also sovereign and not to be trifled with or taken for granted.

DECISION TIME

I fully understand that sometimes these kinds of debates make people angry. That anger is expressed in the students whose worldview demonstrates an intolerance of religion.[62] But everyone must choose. The choice is eternal life or eternal death. No one who chooses Christ need ignore the concerns of this world. But everyone who ignores Christ should be concerned about what awaits them in eternity.

POSTLUDE - A MESSAGE TO SCIENTISTS

I felt that there are many things I'd like to say in this book that would have been too much for the story to bear, but that are related to the content of the story in a significant way. Adding all that material would have made the story too complicated. There are many Christian scientists who have written about science from a Christian worldview. I am just one person who has had many years of experience with both Christianity and science. Over the years, I have formed some thoughts based on observations.

This chapter is my sincere attempt to express the continuity of the Christian worldview with science. When one understands that the Bible complements what we can learn through science, then one can better appreciate both without rejecting either.

One way we can help people appreciate the place of Christianity in a science-oriented world is to understand the consistency of the Christian worldview to life. This book makes no attempt to address all the questions people have about the Bible. However, looking at the overall picture, one can see the consistency between faith and reason as expressed in Christian doctrine. That consistency matches how we think regarding natural science in that observation and faith come together to give us knowledge.

People believe that nature has a truth to it that can be trusted and dis-

---

[61] Jeremiah 18:1-12.
[62] Such anger toward the demands of Christ is seen in many ways by many different groups throughout history and today.

covered. Similarly, Christians believe that God has revealed to us a Truth in Scripture about Himself and ourselves that can be trusted and discovered. This is because the God of nature creates consistency in all He makes and in all He graciously reveals to us. Furthermore, discovering more about God through Scripture is a far more satisfying scientific inquiry than inquiring into nature alone. Even a child can make great progress in understanding God through Scripture.

Knowing God and knowing ourselves in a deep and satisfying way by God's revelation in the Bible does not require a PhD to achieve.

I mention faith as the means of obtaining God's forgiveness and gift of righteousness. This thought is called the doctrine of justification. It reveals to us that God can be both just and the one who justifies us because of the work of Jesus on the cross.[63] The Apostle Paul had claim to significant personal righteousness, that many would consider contributes to their salvation, but which he rejects in favor of the work of Christ on his behalf.[64] We cannot boast in ourselves because of our sins.[65] All our boasting must be in God alone and in what He has done for us.[66]

Figures 1 and 2 below illustrate the view of reality this book identifies. First, when the Triune God of the Bible is the ultimate authority for reality, then God is our ultimate trust. The result is receiving the gift of God's righteousness rather than trying to establish our own.

---

[63] "God presented him as the mercy seat [propitiation, or place of atonement] by his blood, through faith, to demonstrate his righteousness, because in his restraint God passed over the sins previously committed. God presented him to demonstrate his righteousness at the present time, so that he would be just and justify the one who has faith in Jesus" (Romans 3:25-26).

[64] "More than that, I also consider everything to be a loss in view of the surpassing value of knowing Christ Jesus my Lord. Because of him I have suffered the loss of all things and consider them as dung, so that I may gain Christ and be found in him, not having a righteousness of my own from the law, but one that is through faith in Christ —the righteousness from God based on faith" (Philippians 3:8-9).

[65] "What a wretched man I am! Who will rescue me from this body of death? Thanks be to God through Jesus Christ our Lord!" (Romans 7:24-25a).

[66] "God has chosen what is insignificant and despised in the world—what is viewed as nothing—to bring to nothing what is viewed as something, so that no one may boast in his presence. It is from him that you are in Christ Jesus, who became wisdom from God for us—our righteousness, sanctification, and redemption—in order that, as it is written: Let the one who boasts, boast in the Lord" (1 Corinthians 1:28-31).

In the diagrams below we see "Moral" and "Natural" categories. These refer to the laws contained in those categories. Natural Law is something God has given us the ability to discover through science. No doubt He did this for our joy and for the glory He should rightly receive as we honor His wisdom and power in creation. Moral Law can be discovered only to the extent that we observe our own behavior. The moral laws of God are imprinted into human nature by God's design. But sin clouds our understanding, and self is always vying for ultimate authority. Therefore, for certainty and authority, Moral Law must be revealed. God did that so that we can rightly see ourselves as sinners in need of a Savior God Himself.[67]

It is also important to point out that one element of true biblical conversion is that God will write His laws upon the heart.[68] This is a supernatural transformation of the heart by God's Spirit.[69] The result is that a person comes to truly know the Lord![70] This experience is God's way of restoring the fallen human heart. God begins to transform a person from being a lawbreaker to being one humbly seeking to obey His commandments from the heart.[71]

---

[67] "Why, then, was the law given? It was added for the sake of transgressions…" (Galatians 3:19a). Also, "The law, then, was our guardian until Christ, so that we could be justified by faith." (Verse 24).

[68] "'Instead, this is the covenant I will make with the house of Israel after those days'—the Lord's declaration. 'I will put my teaching within them and write it on their hearts. I will be their God, and they will be my people'" (Jeremiah 31:33).

[69] "I will give you a new heart and put a new spirit within you; I will remove your heart of stone and give you a heart of flesh" (Ezekiel 36:26).

[70] "'No longer will one teach his neighbor or his brother, saying, 'Know the Lord,' for they will all know me, from the least to the greatest of them'—this is the Lord's declaration. 'For I will forgive their iniquity and never again remember their sin'" (Jeremiah 31:34).

[71] "For this is what love for God is: to keep his commands. And his commands are not a burden" (1 John 5:3).

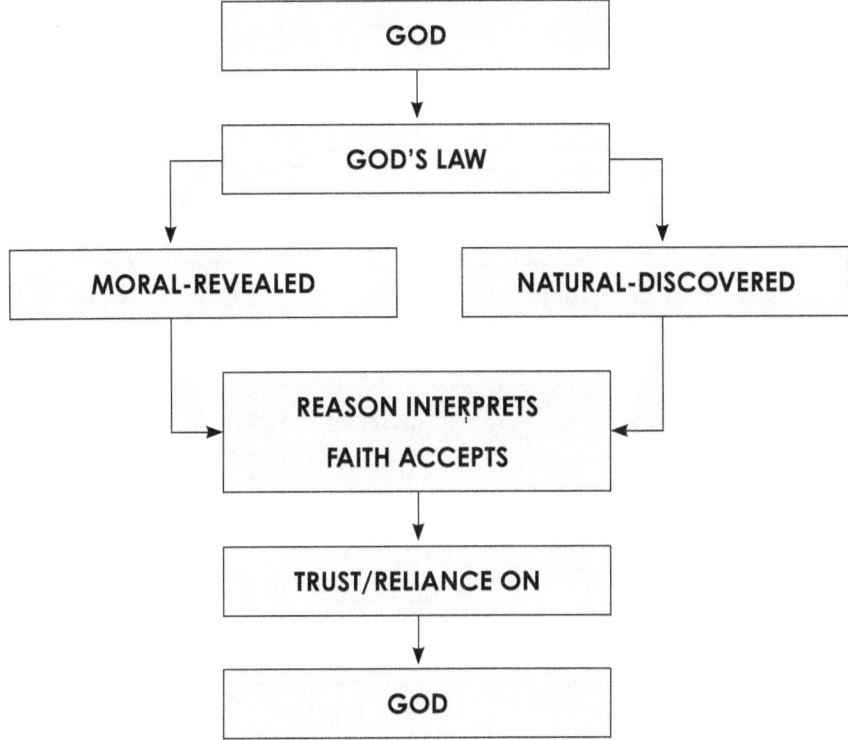

Figure 1 – When God is the ultimate authority to determine reality, one's view of life honors God through faith, resulting in God justifying the sinner with His righteousness.

However, when mankind is the starting point through a material view of reality, then self is the ultimate trust. The result is an attempt at self-justification through self-righteousness. One ultimately depends upon self, supported and buttressed by a self-oriented view of morality.

Yet, one can never truly escape the reality of God's Law as the standard of morality He will use to judge us. Nor can we escape God Himself as the Judge of where we put our ultimate trust.

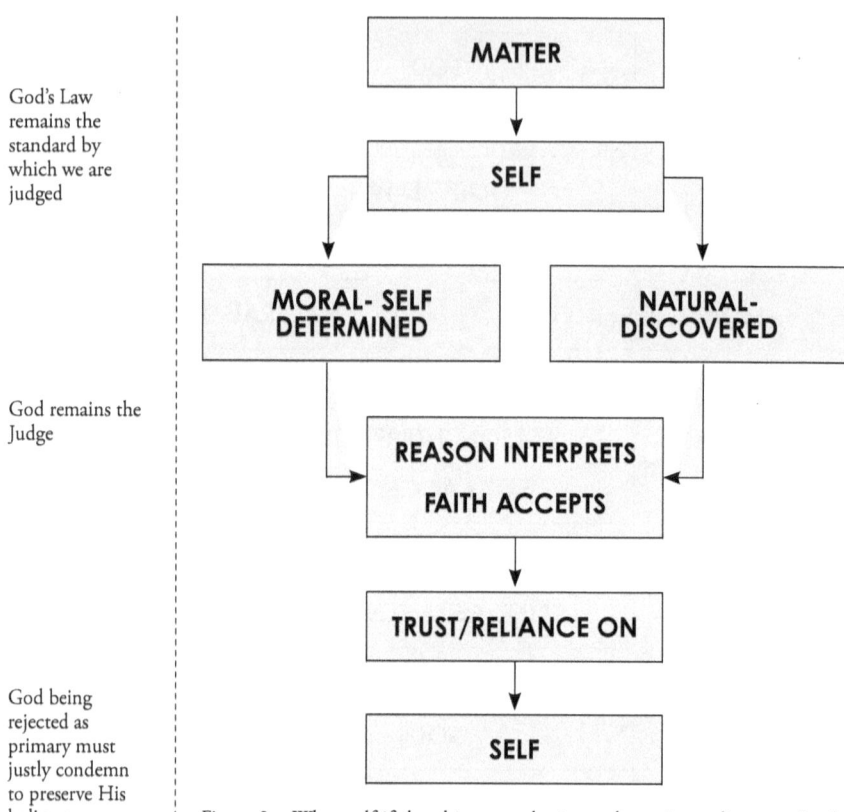

God's Law remains the standard by which we are judged

God remains the Judge

God being rejected as primary must justly condemn to preserve His holiness

Figure 2 – When self if the ultimate authority to determine reality, one simply interprets life to affirm self, resulting in self-justification by self-righteousness.

Note further in these diagrams the role of "reason" and "faith." They work together to establish our sense of authority which leads to trust and reliance upon something. This goes back to what I said in the story about how we view life: our beliefs form our worldview, that determines our behavior and how we see the world, we then live our lives testing those beliefs, and we change our beliefs or our interpretation of those beliefs to suit ourselves. This circular thinking is at the heart of our human nature, but it cannot lead to salvation when God is not the ultimate and fundamental reference point through His revelation in the Bible, because we will be placing our ultimate trust in ourselves.

SUMMARY REMARKS

The Christian message fits the data. What do I mean by that? Consider the following summary thoughts. They express that the Christian message in the Bible is a reasonable answer to the observations of life. What's more, the Christian message, being based on revelation, provides mankind with hope that's rooted in God and not ourselves.

1) **People are vastly different than animals in how we interpret the world, how we concern ourselves with morality, and how we inquire philosophically, scientifically, and theologically about reality**
   a. This is evidence of mankind being made differently than animals[72]
   b. The Bible reveals we are made in God's image to reflect His character and attributes, as well as to know Him and learn from Him[73]

2) **People assert their will by creating their own standards to live by**
   a. This is evidence of a nature focused on self, disconnected from a spiritual relationship to God[74]
   b. The Bible reveals we are fallen creatures with a sinful nature that leads to rebellion against God and His Laws[75]
   c. The Bible also reveals the influence of fallen angels, called devils, who are also in rebellion against God and who have a profound effect on fallen humans[76]

3) **People exhibit evil through such attitudes as cruelty, bigotry, deceit, deception, lying, hatred, violence, stealing, coveting, immorality, lawlessness, false religion, and hypocrisy**
   a. This is evidence of mankind's fallen nature and need for a changed (renewed) heart[77]
   b. The Bible reveals that evil comes from within us, from our heart, and this defiles us before God, placing us under God's just wrath by nature[78]
   c. The Bible reveals that God alone can change the heart and He promises to do so[79] with those who turn to Him through His Son[80]

---

[72] Psalm 8; Genesis 2:19.
[73] Genesis 1:26-30; 2:15-17.
[74] John 17:25.
[75] Romans 3:23.
[76] Ephesians 2:1-2.
[77] Mark 7:20-23.
[78] Ephesians 2:3.
[79] Jeremiah 31:33; Ezekiel 36:26.
[80] Titus 3:4-7.

4) **People invent their own religions that allow them to achieve "salvation" by their own efforts**
   a. This is evidence of mankind's wondering from God, of not knowing God, of lostness and misdirection, confusion, and of seeking to establish our own righteousness[81]
   b. The Bible reveals that our own righteousness is considered as "filthy rags"[82] by God so that we cannot be saved by them, but are in need of God to do for us by His grace what we cannot do for ourselves[83]

The Bible rightly interprets the evidence of human behavior and presents God's remedy for it. It is truly an awesome book written through the Spirit of an awesome God. However, so long as people ignore God's revealed explanation and instructions, then they will continue to grope in darkness, being subject to future judgment that leaves them without hope because they have turned their backs on God.

As I said at the start of this book, I'm not trying to win an argument here. These are eternal matters that bear upon our souls. I'm merely urging everyone who reads this to come to Christ. The truth is a radical change is required for us to be saved!

Therefore, I hope you will turn from your own way and trust Christ. I hope you can understand why faith *and* repentance go together in the Christian message. As we trust Jesus as our Savior to give us the salvation that God alone can provide, we simultaneously turn from our own way back to God and follow Jesus as our Lord, exhibiting a new heart that now seeks to humbly love and serve God.

To God be all the glory for His marvelous ways and His great mercy and grace to us sinners!

> *"For God loved the world in this way: He gave his one and only Son, so that everyone who believes in him will not perish but have eternal life." (John 3:16)*

---

[81] Romans 3:10, 10:3.
[82] Isaiah 64:6.
[83] Romans 8:3-4.

PERSONAL TESTIMONY OF SALVATION

I grew up attending a Roman Catholic Church with my family. Throughout my youth, my conscience was impressed by God's Ten Commandments. I went to Confession about once a year, was catechized and confirmed, although the only Scripture I knew was the Ten Commandments and the Beatitudes. I did not know the Lord, nor did I understand the gospel.

The summer following my freshman year of high school was spiritually traumatic for me. At that time, I was becoming more and more involved in sin with my peers. Then, toward the end of the summer prior to my sophomore year, God began working in my heart and gave me a sense of the "falseness" of what I was doing. It was as though the desire for the things I was doing suddenly left me. Yet I still did not know the Lord. In retrospect, I believe God was drawing me to Himself.

Then, one night in October of my sophomore year of high school, I walked into my bedroom and felt a sense that God was calling me. It was not audible, of course, but He called me in my heart, giving me a strong conviction that I needed to get the family Bible and read it. I had previously only opened the Bible to read it a couple of times, but now I had a desire to start reading the Gospel of John. I read the Scriptures with great attraction until I reached John chapter 3. As I read Jesus' words, "you must be born again," I realized that this was happening to me. Then, when I read John 3:16 (for the first time in my life) I knew that Jesus Christ died for my sins.

From that day on I had a new spiritual life. I knew God, hated my sin, and loved Jesus Christ and the Bible. What the hymn writer Charles Wesley (1707-1788) once wrote was true of me that night,

> *"Thine eye diffused a quickening ray,*
> *I woke, the dungeon flamed with light;*
> *My chains fell off, my heart was free;*
> *I rose, went forth, and followed Thee."*[84]

While in college I ended up at a Baptist church. It was there that I came to a better understanding of God's amazing grace that saved me, and I was humbled to think He would save me for nothing in me, but simply because of His loving grace. It was there that I was baptized as a believer.

---

[84] Public Domain. https://hymnary.org/text/and_can_it_be_that_i_should_gain.

> *"Get up, sleeper, and rise up from the dead, and Christ will shine on you." (Ephesians 5:13b)*

www.ingramcontent.com/pod-product-compliance
Lightning Source LLC
Chambersburg PA
CBHW022009120526
44592CB00034B/761